PIANO · VOCAL · CHORDS

2008 GREATEST Pop & Rock Hits

W9-BFJ-719

★ THE BIGGEST HITS ★ DELUXE ANNUAL EDITION ★ THE GREATEST ARTISTS

CONTENTS

Alfred Publishing Co., Inc.
16320 Roscoe Blvd., Suite 100
P.O. Box 10003
Van Nuys, CA 91410-0003
alfred.com

Copyright © MMVIII by Alfred Publishing Co., Inc.
All rights reserved. Printed in USA.

ISBN-10: 0-7390-5368-X
ISBN-13: 978-0-7390-5368-3

ALMOST LOVER

Words and Music by
ALISON SUDOL

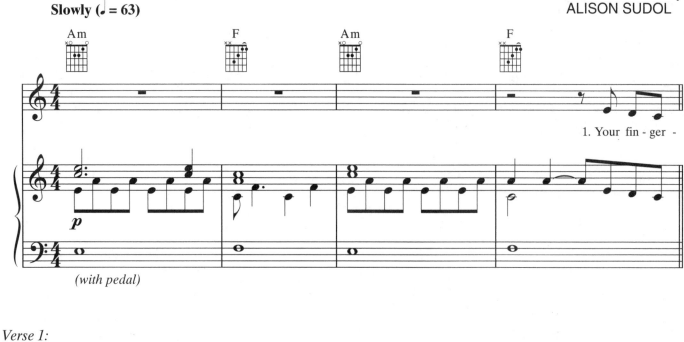

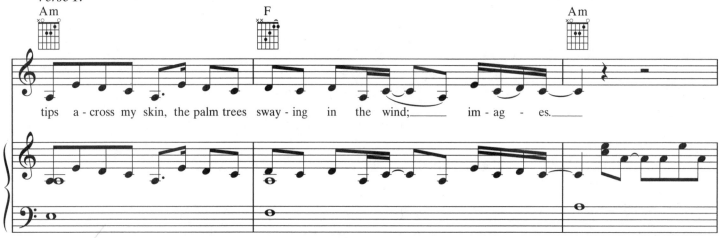

D.S. % al Coda

 Coda

Bridge:

night. I can - not__ wake__ up in the morn - ing with - out you on my mind.__

__ So you're gone__ and I'm__ haunt - ed, and I'll bet you are just__

fine. Did I make it that__ eas - y to walk right in and out of my

life?_____ *Chorus:* Good - bye,__ my al - most lov - er.

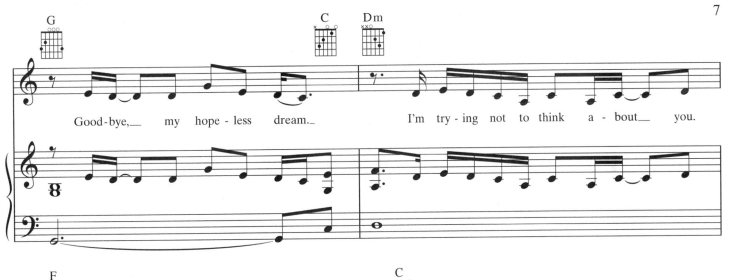

BODYSNATCHERS

Words and Music by
THOMAS YORKE, JONATHAN GREENWOOD, COLIN GREENWOOD,
EDWARD O'BRIEN and PHILIP SELWAY

Bodysnatchers - 8 - 1

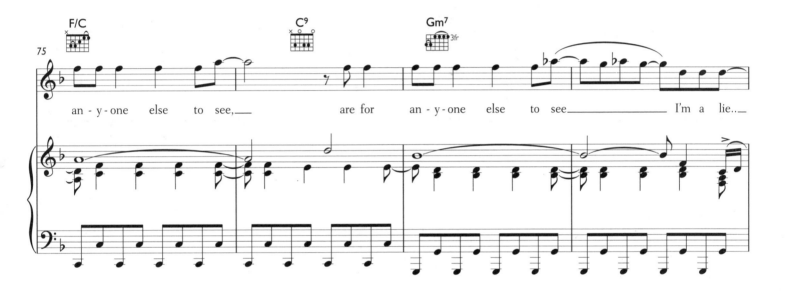

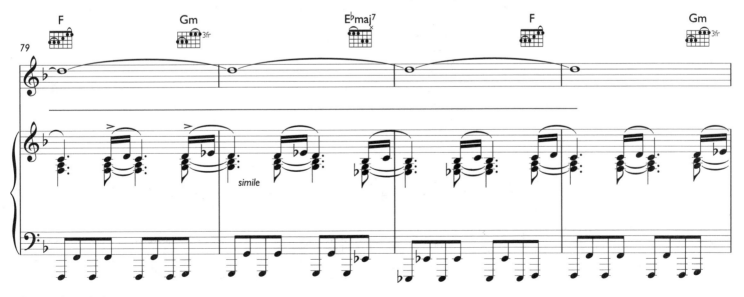

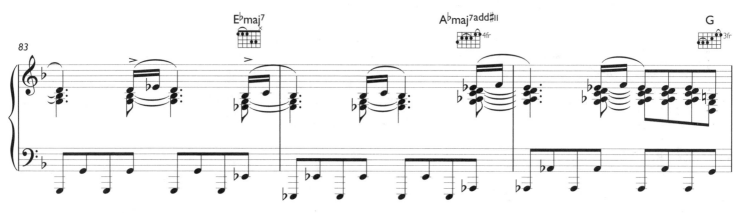

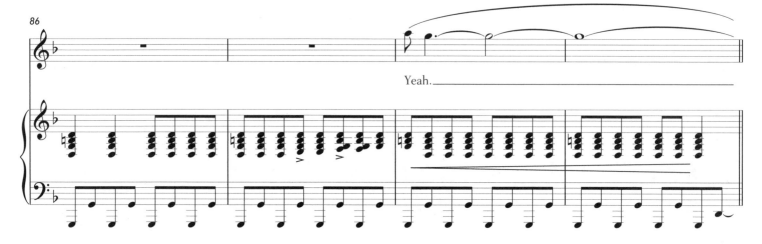

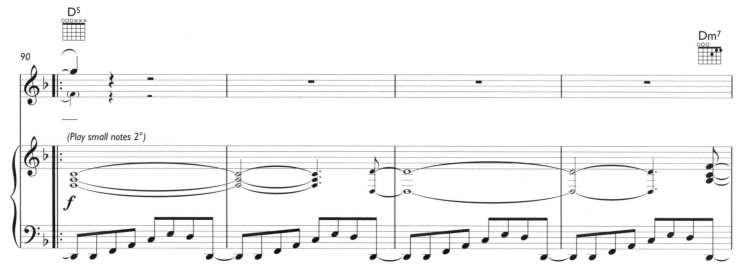

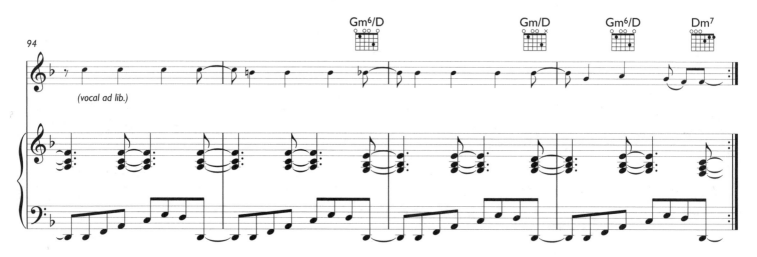

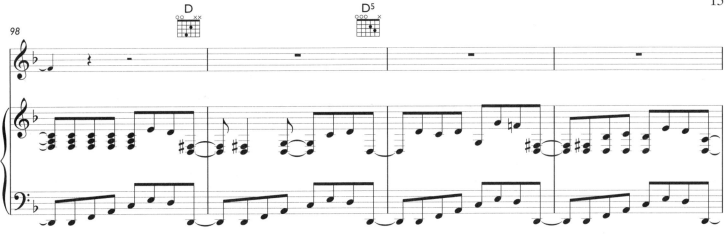

I've seen it coming, I've seen it com - ing, I've seen it com - ing, I've seen it com - ing.

CELEBRATE ME HOME

Lyrics by
KENNY LOGGINS

Music by
KENNY LOGGINS and BOB JAMES

18

CLUMSY

Words and Music by
BOBBY TROUP, WILL ADAMS
and STACY FERGUSON

Clumsy - 8 - 1

now. I'm back in love now, baby. I'm back in love
Can't help it, the girl can't help it. Can't help it, the girl can't help it.
Chorus:
N.C.
C
Dm7/C
now. And now you got me. Oh. Oh.
Can't help it. You got me trip - pin', stum - bl - in',
C
Dm7/C
C
Dm7/C
Oh. No. Clum - sy 'cause I'm fall - in' in
flip - pin', fum - bl - in'.
C
Dm7/C
C
Dm7/C
love. Oh. Oh.
In, in, love, love. You got me slip - pin', tum - bl - in',

28

COME ON, COME OUT

Words and Music by
ALISON SUDOL, LUKAS BURTON
and HAL CRAGIN

Come On, Come Out - 6 - 1

Come on, come out, said, come on, come out. 2. A

Verse 2:

spot in the shade, where or-an-ges fall. A

spot in the shade, a-way from it all.

Chorus:

Watch-ing the sky, you're watch-ing a paint-ing com-ing to life, shift-ing and shap-ing.

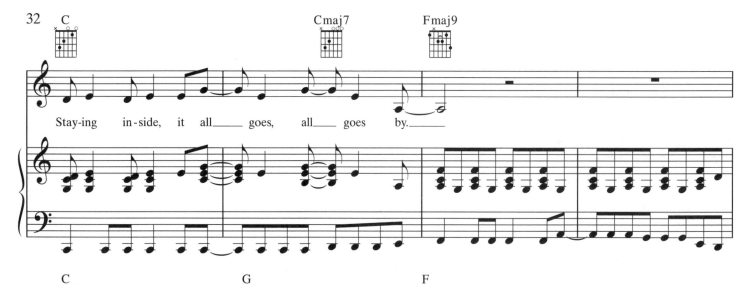

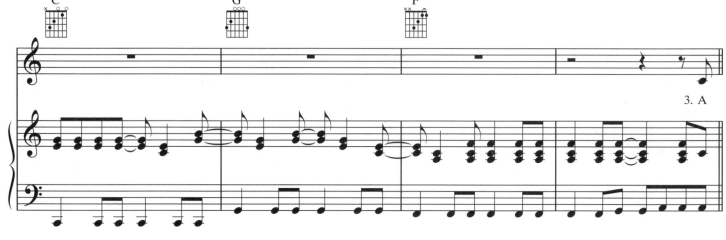

Verse 3:

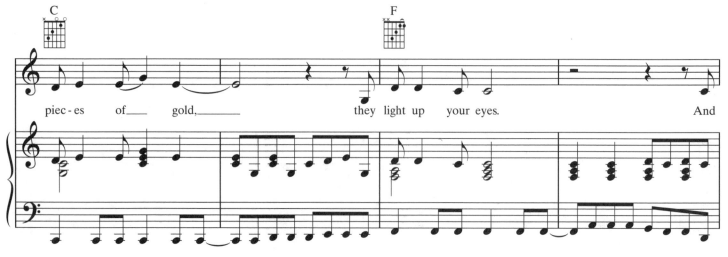

34

Keep it in-side, it all___ goes, all___ goes, all___ goes, all___ goes_ by.___ It

Bridge:

all___ goes___ pass - ing___ by.___ It

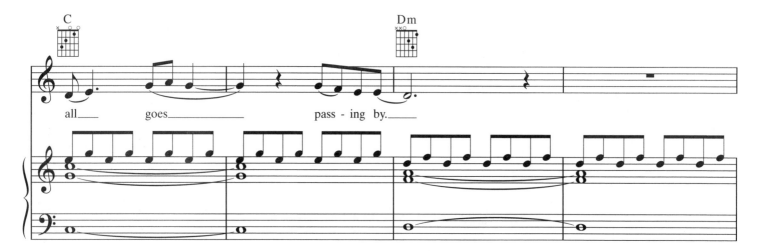

all___ goes___ pass - ing by.___

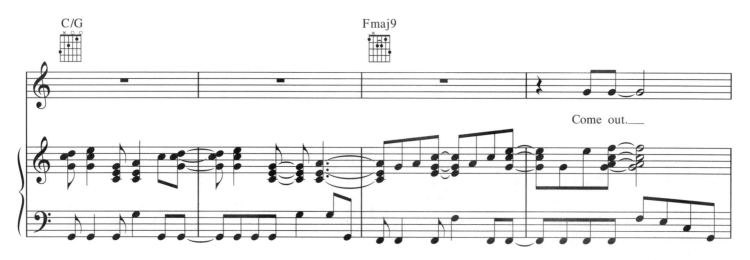

Come out.___

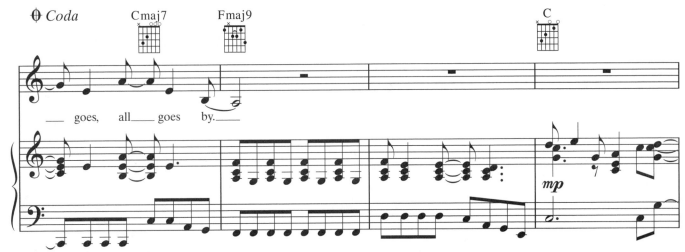

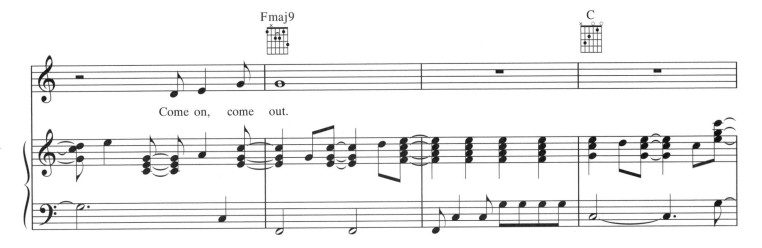

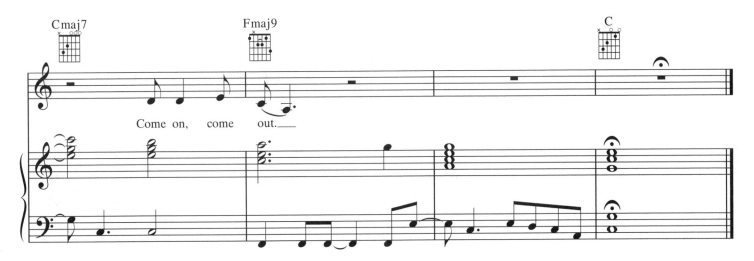

CRUSHCRUSHCRUSH

Words and Music by
HAYLEY WILLIAMS
and JOSH FARRO

*All Gtrs. in Drop D tuning, down 1/2 step:

⑥ = D♭ ③ = G♭
⑤ = A♭ ② = B♭
④ = D♭ ① = E♭

Moderately fast ♩ = 138

Verse:

1. I got a lot___ to say___ to you,   yeah,
(2.) you wan-na play___ it like___ a game,   well,

I got a lot___ to say.___   I no-ticed your eyes___ are al-
come on, come on, let's play.___   'Cause I'd rath-er waste___ my

ways glued___ to me,   keep-ing them here___ and it makes___ no sense___ at___ all.
___ pre-tend-ing than have to for-get___ you for one___ whole min-ute.

*B♯ = C♮

CrushCrushCrush - 6 - 1

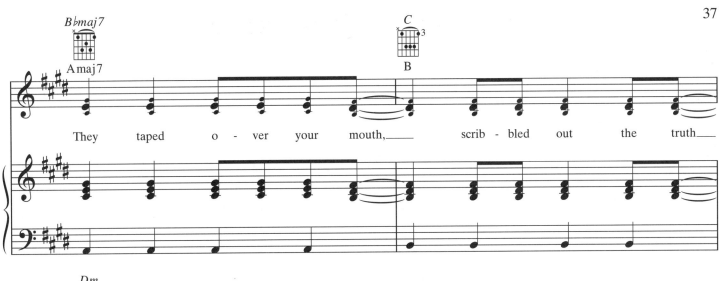

They taped o - ver your mouth,___ scrib - bled out the truth___

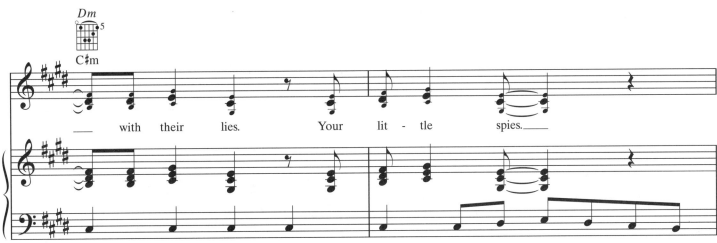

___ with their lies. Your lit - tle spies.___

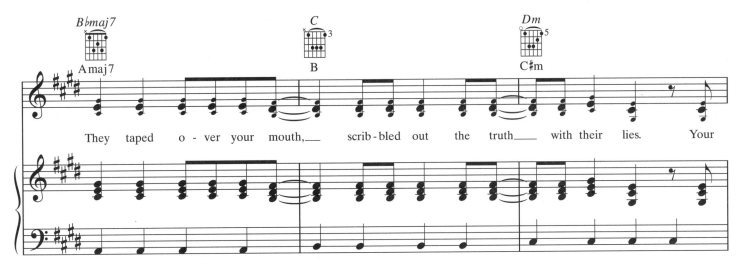

They taped o - ver your mouth,___ scrib - bled out the truth___ with their lies. Your

lit - tle spies.___

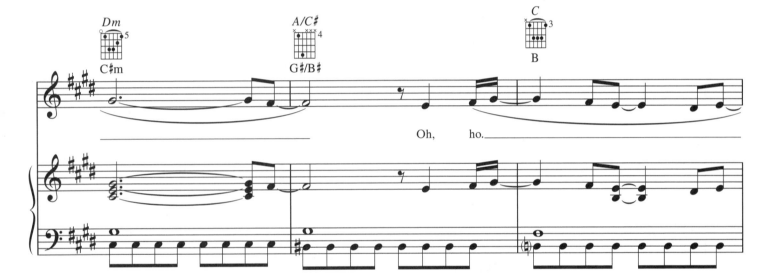

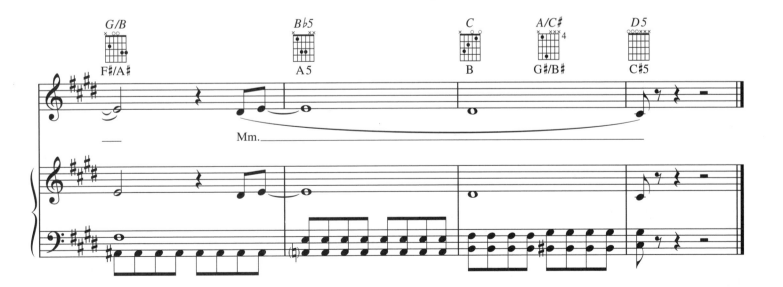

DON'T STOP THE MUSIC

Words and Music by
MICHAEL JACKSON, MIKKEL STORLEER ERIKSEN,
TOR ERIK HERMANSEN and FRANKIE STORM

cred - i - ble.____ If you don't have to go,____ don't.____
has to know.____ This is a pri - vate show,____ oh.____

Do you know what you start-ed?

I just came here to par - ty, but now we're rock-in' on the dance floor, act-in' naugh-ty.

F#m

Your hand's a-round my waist. Just let the mu-sic play. We're hand in hand, chest to

𝄋 *Chorus:*

D

chest, and now we're face to face. I wan - na take you____ a - way. Let's es - cape in - to the

F#m

mu - sic.___ D J, let___ it play. I just can't re - fuse it. Like the way you

do this. Keep on rock - in' to it. Please don't stop the, please don't stop the mu - sic.

D

I wan - na take you___ a - way. Let's es-cape in - to the mu - sic.___ D J, let___ it

F#m

play. I just can't re - fuse it. Like the way you do this. Keep on rock - in'

1.

to it. Please don't stop the, please don't stop the, please don't stop the

2.3.   D

please don't stop the, please don't stop the mu - sic.

Ma ma   se ma ma sa ma ma___ coo sa,___ ma ma

se ma ma sa ma ma___ coo sa.   Ma ma   se ma ma sa ma ma___ coo sa,___ ma ma

F#m

Please don't   stop the   mu -   sic.

se ma ma sa ma ma___ coo sa.   Ma ma   se ma ma   sa ma ma___ coo sa,___ ma ma

To Coda ⊕

se ma ma sa ma ma___ coo sa. Ma ma se ma ma sa ma ma___ coo sa,___ ma ma

N.C.

Please don't stop the mu - sic.

se ma ma sa ma ma___ coo sa. Ma ma se ma ma sa ma ma___ coo sa,___ ma ma

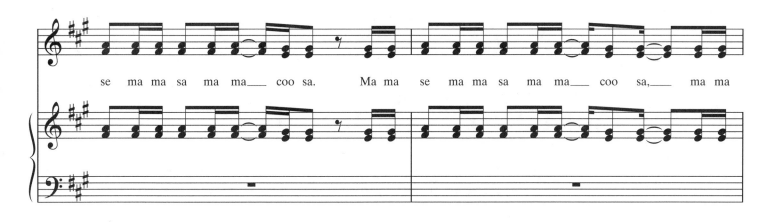

se ma ma sa ma ma___ coo sa. Ma ma se ma ma sa ma ma___ coo sa,___ ma ma

Please don't stop the mu - sic.___

se ma ma sa ma ma___ coo sa. Ma ma se ma ma sa ma ma___ coo sa,___ ma ma

se ma ma sa ma ma____ coo sa. Ma ma se ma ma sa ma ma____ coo sa,____ ma ma se ma ma sa ma ma____ coo sa.

⊕ *Coda*

N.C.

Please don't stop the mu - sic.
se ma ma sa ma ma____ coo sa. Ma ma se ma ma sa ma ma____ coo sa,____ ma ma

se ma ma sa ma ma____ coo sa. Ma ma se ma ma sa ma ma____ coo sa,____ ma ma

Please don't stop the mu - sic.
se ma ma sa ma ma____ coo sa.

EVERYTHING

Words and Music by
MICHAEL BUBLÉ, ALAN CHANG
and AMY FOSTER-GILLIES

Chorus:

zy___ life,___ and through these cra - zy times,___ ___ it's you,___ it's you.___ You make me sing.___ You're ev - 'ry line,___ ___ you're ev - 'ry word,___ you're ev - 'ry - thing.___

2. You're a car -

Chorus:

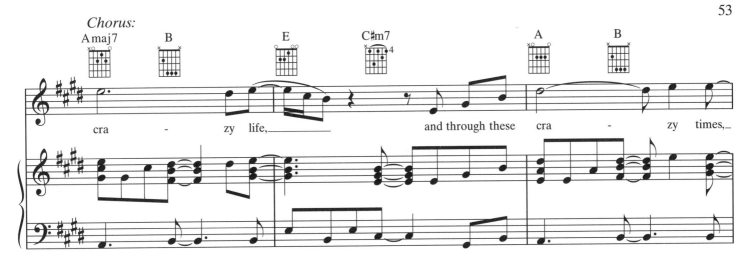

cra - zy life,_____ and through these cra - zy times,_

___ it's you,__ it's you.__ You make me sing.__ You're ev - 'ry line,_

___ you're ev - 'ry word,_ you're ev - 'ry - thing._____

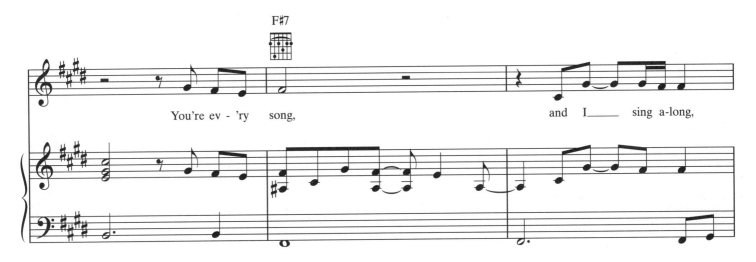

You're ev - 'ry song, and I___ sing a - long,

'cause you're my ev - 'ry - thing._____

So la_____ la

la   la   la   la   la._____   So

Freely

la_____ la   la   la   la la la la_____ la la la._____

FAKE IT

Music and Lyrics by
SHAUN MORGAN, DALE STEWART
and JOHN HUMPHREY

All Gtrs. in Drop D, down one whole step:
⑥ = C   ③ = F
⑤ = G   ② = A
④ = C   ① = D

1.3. Who's to know__ if your soul will fade at all?__ The
2. You should know__ that your lies won't hide your flaws.__ No

one you sold to fool the world.__ You lost your self-es-teem a-long__ the way,__
sense in hid-ing all of yours.__ You gave up on your dreams a-long__ the way,__

Pre-chorus:

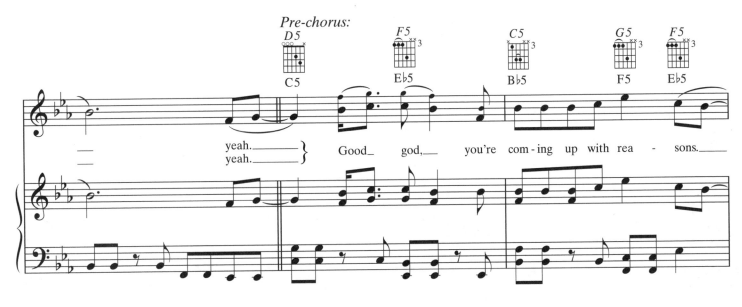

__ yeah.__ } Good__ god,__ you're com-ing up with rea-sons.__
__ yeah.__

Fake It - 5 - 1

56

Bridge:

I can fake with the best of an - y - one,__ I can fake with the

best of them all. I can fake with the best of an - y - one,__

D.C. al Coda

I can fake it all._____

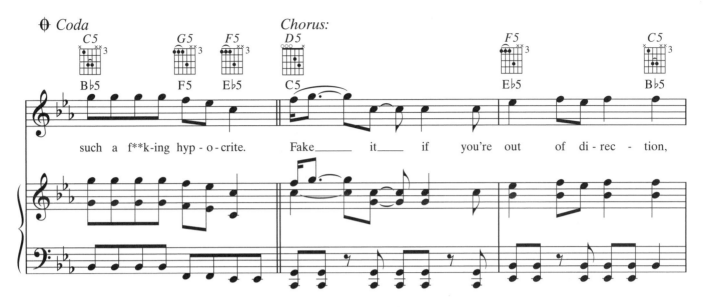

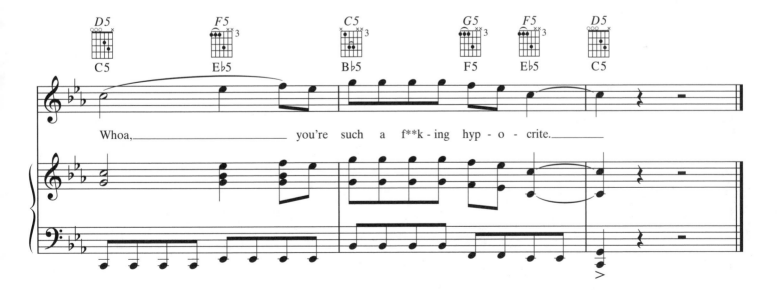

GIRLS IN THEIR SUMMER CLOTHES

Words and Music by
BRUCE SPRINGSTEEN

Moderately ♩ = 120

1. Well, the street-lights shine___

Verse 1:

down on Bless - ing Av - e - nue.___   Lov-ers, they walk by,___

hold-ing hands two by two.___   A breeze cross-es the porch;___

Girls in Their Summer Clothes - 7 - 1

Verse 2:

Chorus:

Bridge:

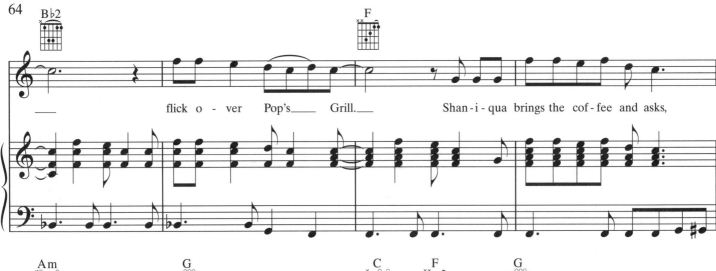

flick o - ver Pop's___ Grill.___ Shan-i-qua brings the cof-fee and asks,

"Fill?" and says, "Pen-ny for your thoughts now, my boy, Bill."___ 3. She went a - way;___

Verse 3:

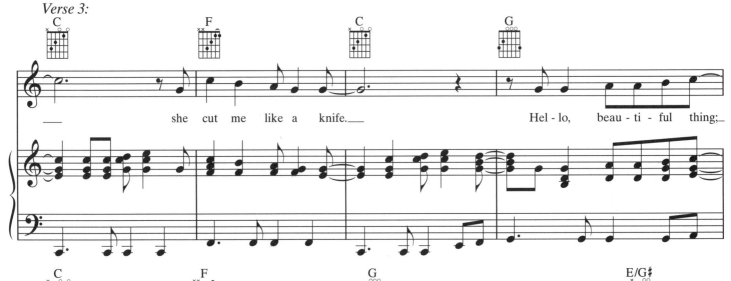

___ she cut me like a knife.___ Hel - lo, beau - ti - ful thing;___

___ may-be you could save my life.___ In just a glance,___

down here on Mag-ic Street,___ love's a fool's dance;___

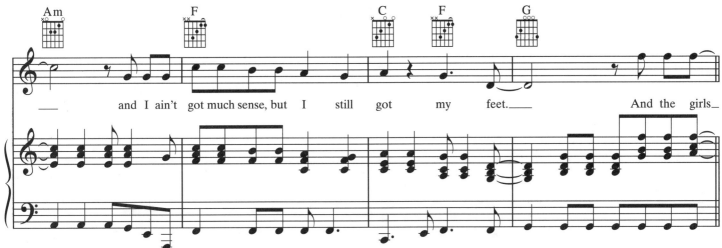

___ and I ain't got much sense, but I still got my feet.___ And the girls___

Chorus:

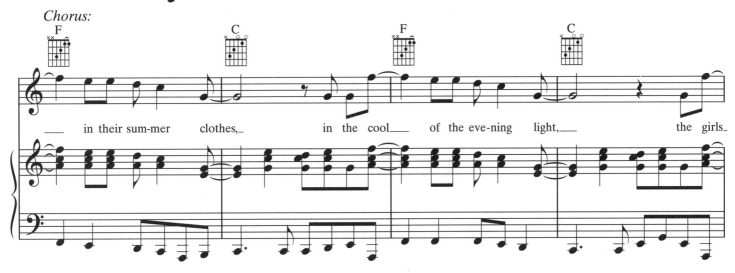

___ in their sum-mer clothes,___ in the cool___ of the eve-ning light,___ the girls___

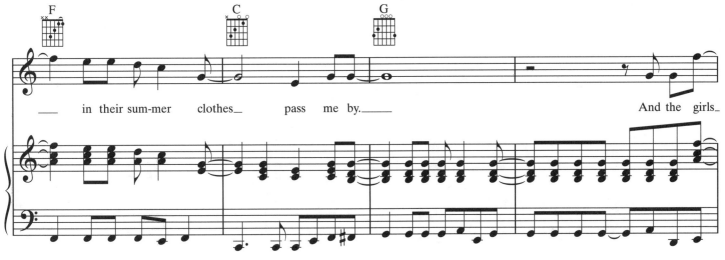

___ in their sum-mer clothes___ pass me by._____ And the girls___

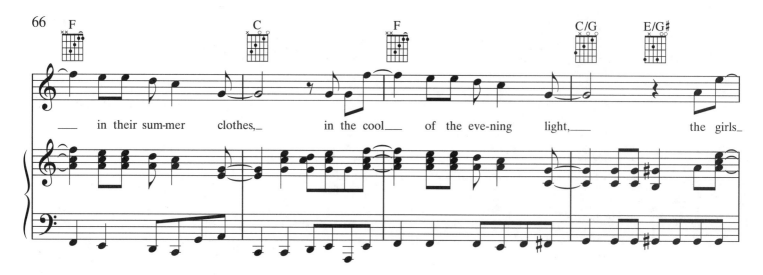

in their sum-mer clothes,__ in the cool__ of the eve-ning light,__ the girls__

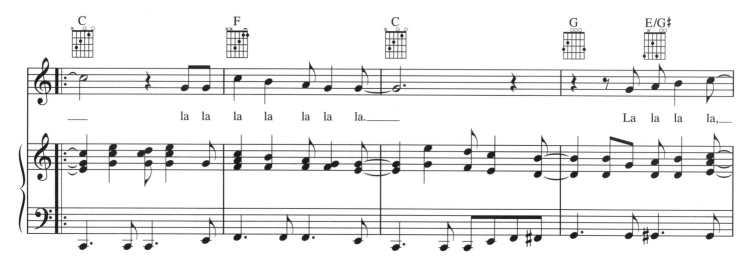

__ in their sum-mer clothes__ pass me by._____ La la la,__

__ la la la la la la la._____ La la la la,__

Repeat ad lib. and fade

__ la la la la la la la._____ La la la,__

GOODBYE PHILADELPHIA

Words and Music by
PETER CINCOTTI and JOHN BETTIS

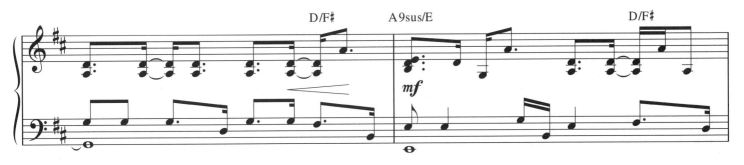

Verse:

1. Just like Phil - a - del - phi - a,

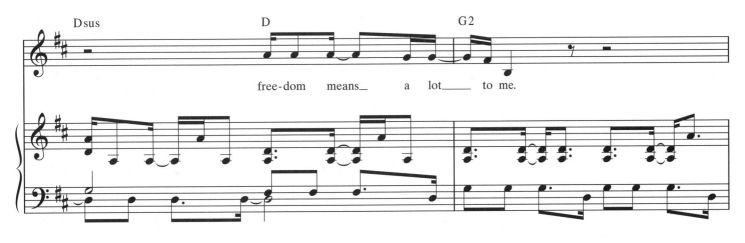

free-dom means___ a lot___ to me.

Goodbye Philadelphia - 9 - 1

68

In be-tween_ the place_ I've been_

and where I'm go-in',

I can see_ A-mer-i-ca

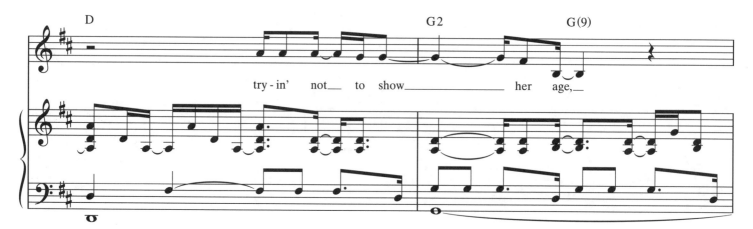

try-in' not_ to show_ her age,_

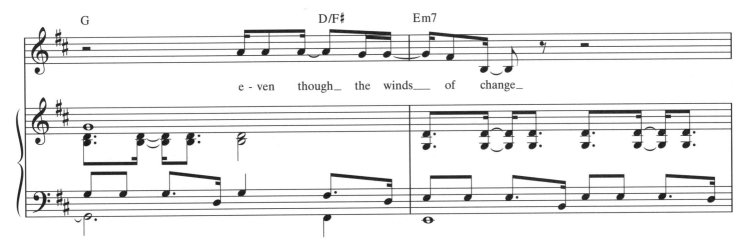

e - ven though_ the winds_ of change_

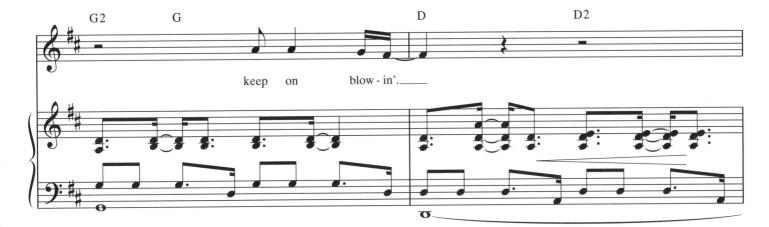

keep on blow - in'.____

℁ *Chorus:*

And I would lay_____ your bod-y down_ and rock_ your tears_

___ a - way.___ But it's much_ too late_ for now_ to be_ like yes-

70

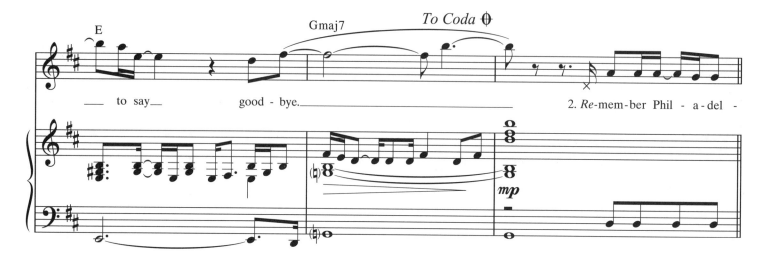

Verse 2:

til it makes

noth - ing of___ you.___

D.S. % al Coda

— And I would lay___

Coda

(Instrumental)

mp

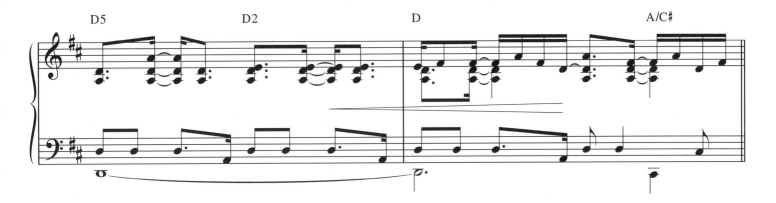

Bridge:

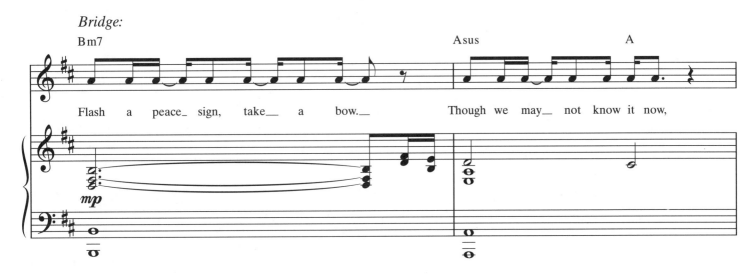

Flash a peace_ sign, take_ a bow._ Though we may_ not know it now,

things are_ nev - er gon - na be_____ the same._____

ter-day. And the time___ is run-ning out,___ and we___ still have_

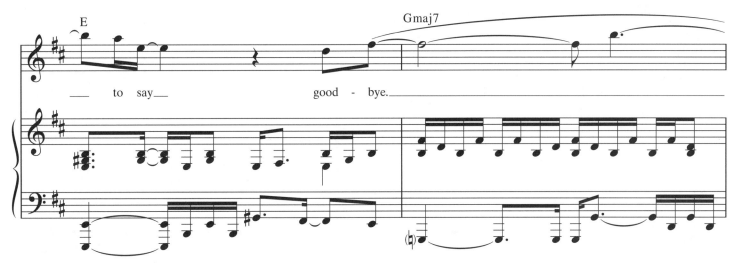

___ to say___ good - bye.___

___ Good - bye.___ Good-bye._

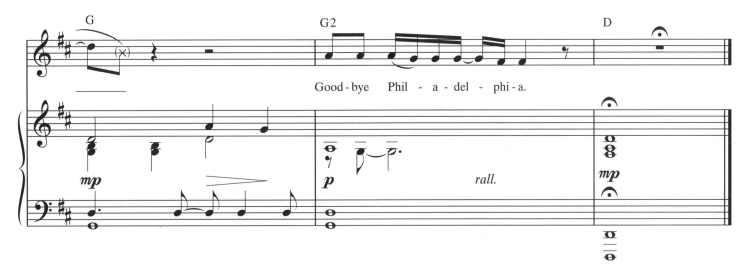

Good-bye Phil - a - del - phi - a.

HEY THERE DELILAH

Words and Music by
TOM HIGGENSON

Moderately ♩ = 108

Verses 1 & 2:

1. Hey there, De - li - lah, what's_ it like in New_ York Cit - y? I'm a thou-
2. Hey there, De - li - lah, I_ know times are get - ting hard, but just be - lieve_

sand miles a - way,_ but, girl,_ to - night_ you look so pret - ty, yes, you do.
__ me, girl, some-day_ I'll pay_ the bills_ with this gui - tar, we'll have it good.

Hey There Delilah - 7 - 1

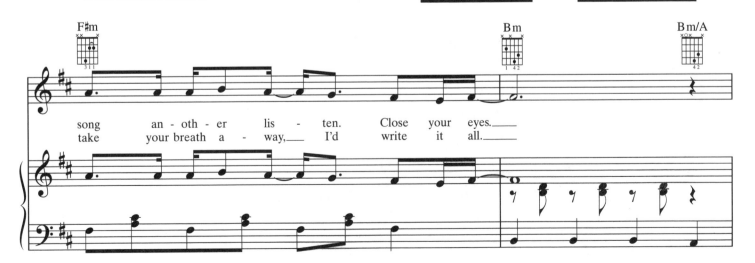

Bridge:

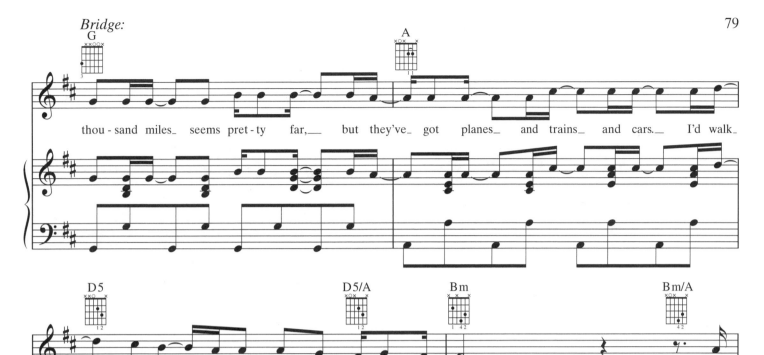

thou-sand miles_ seems pret-ty far,_ but they've_ got planes_ and trains_ and cars._ I'd walk_

_ to you_ if I had no oth-er way._ Our

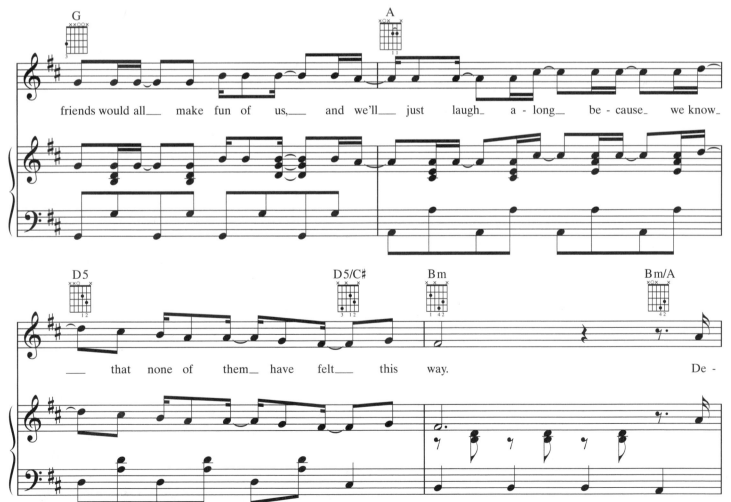

friends would all_ make fun of us,_ and we'll_ just laugh_ a-long_ be-cause_ we know_

_ that none of them_ have felt_ this way. De-

li - lah, I can prom-ise you___ that by___ the time___ we___ get through,___ the world___

___ will nev - er, ev - er be the same,_____ and you're to blame.___

A

Verse 3:

3. Hey there, De - li - lah, you be good___ and don't you miss___ me. Two more

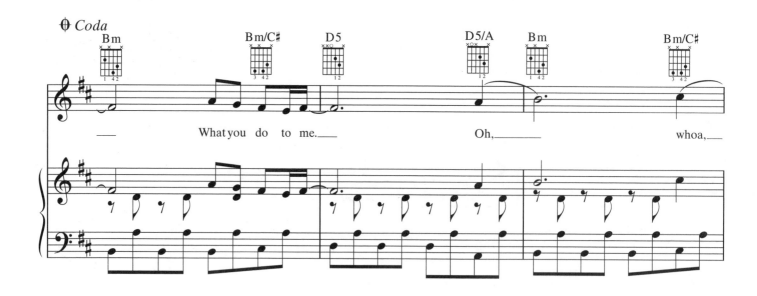

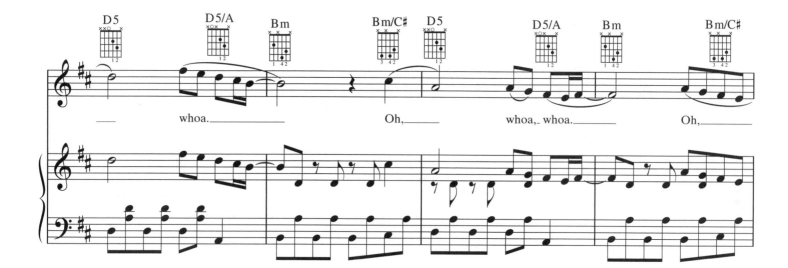

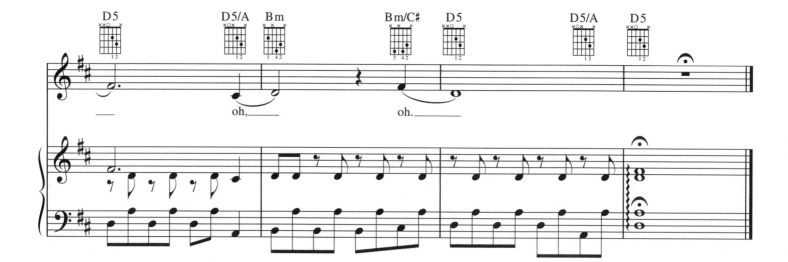

I'LL KEEP YOUR MEMORY VAGUE

Music and Lyrics by
SCOTT ANDERSON, SEAN ANDERSON,
RICH BEDDOE, JAMES BLACK
and RICK JACKETT

Moderately slow ♩ = 80

Verse 1:

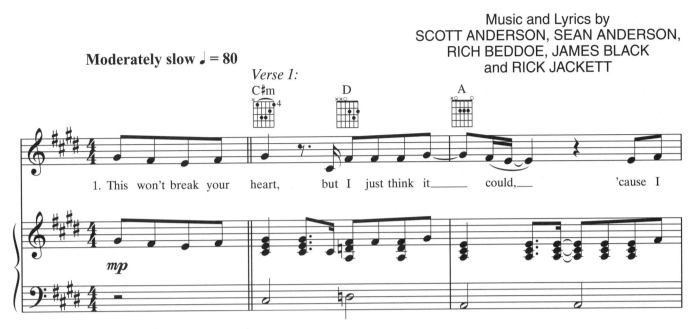

1. This won't break your heart, but I just think it____ could,____ 'cause I

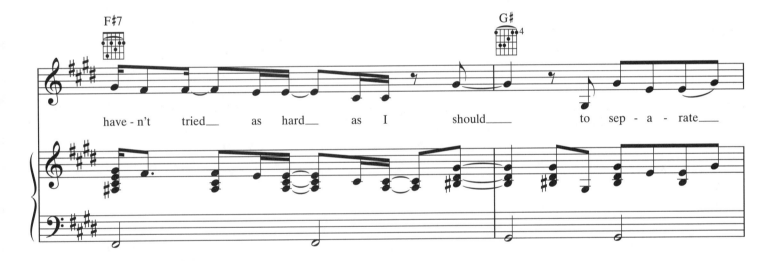

have-n't tried____ as hard____ as I should____ to sep-a-rate____

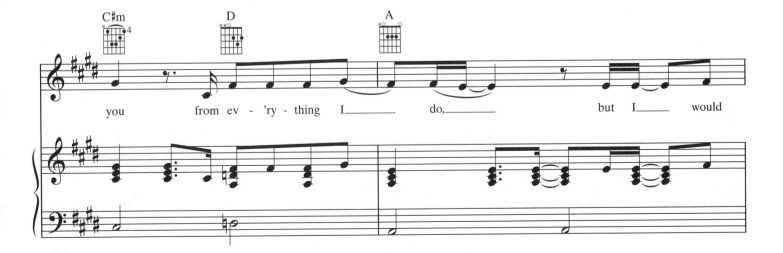

you from ev-'ry-thing I____ do,____ but I____ would

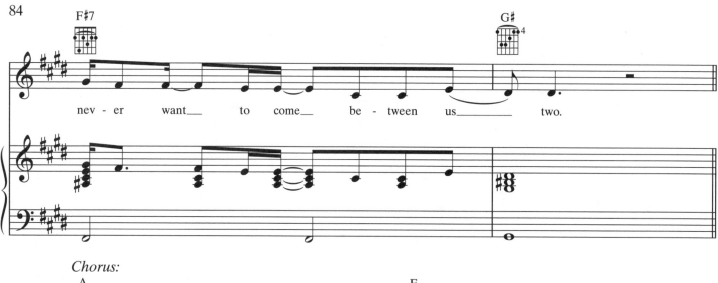

nev - er want___ to come___ be - tween us_____ two.

Chorus:

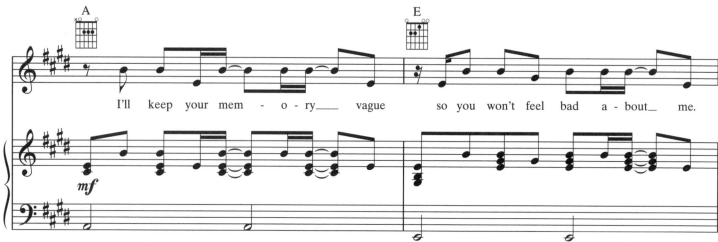

I'll keep your mem - o - ry___ vague so you won't feel bad a - bout__ me.

I'll say the things__ that you__ said some - times so it re - minds__ me.

I'll keep your mem - o - ry___ vague so you won't feel bad a - bout__ me.

I'll say the things_ that you_ said some - times so it re - minds_ me._

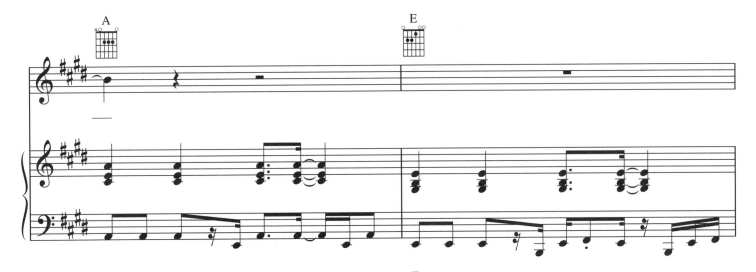

2. But now I'm think - in'

Verse 2:

back to what I said be - fore._____ I hope_ your

heart won't have to hurt__ an - y - more,__ 'cause it's real - ly not that__

__ sad__ from__ here,__ be - cause the

mo - ments I can feel you__ near,__ they keep you

close to me,__ my dear,__ and if they ev - er be - come__ too clear...__

To Coda ⊕

Bridge:

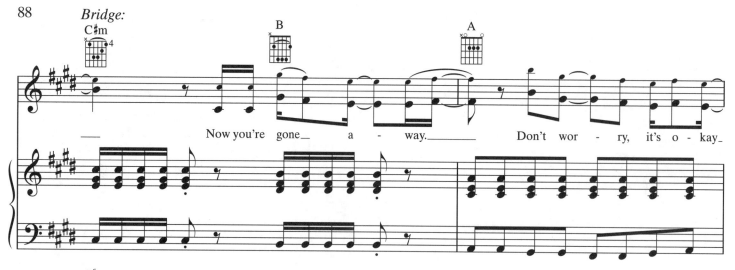

Now you're gone___ a - way.___ Don't wor - ry, it's o - kay_

that you're gone___ a - way.___

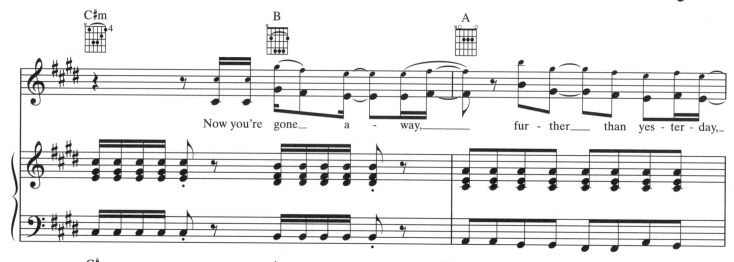

Now you're gone___ a - way,___ fur - ther___ than yes - ter - day,_

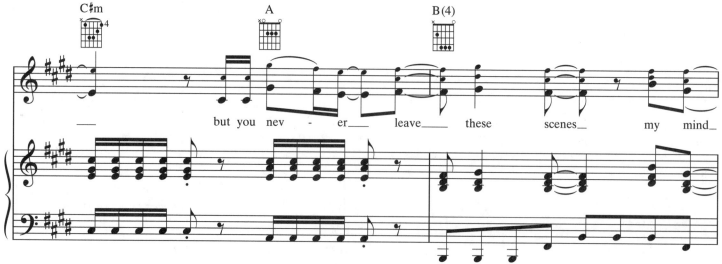

but you nev - er leave___ these scenes___ my mind_

D.S. % al Coda   ⊕ *Coda*

world?

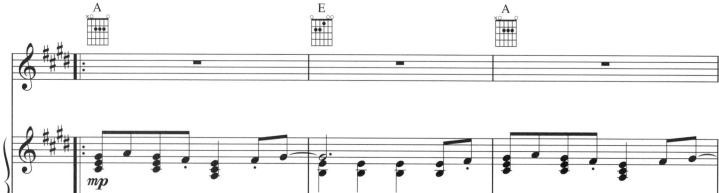

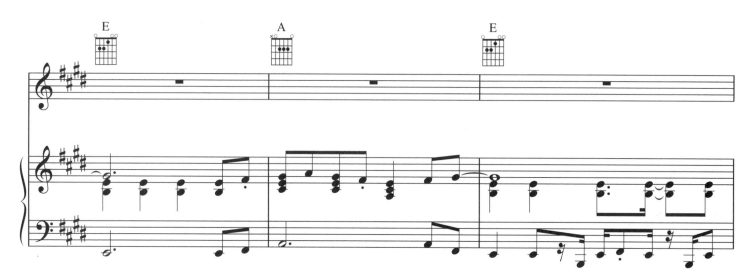

Repeat ad lib. and fade

IN LOVE WITH A GIRL

Words and Music by
GAVIN DeGRAW

In Love With a Girl - 6 - 1

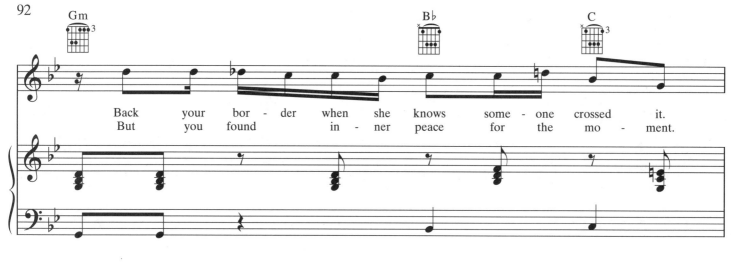

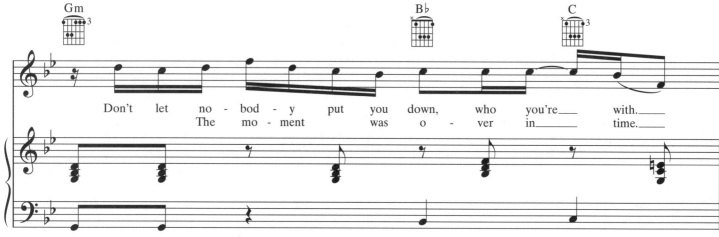

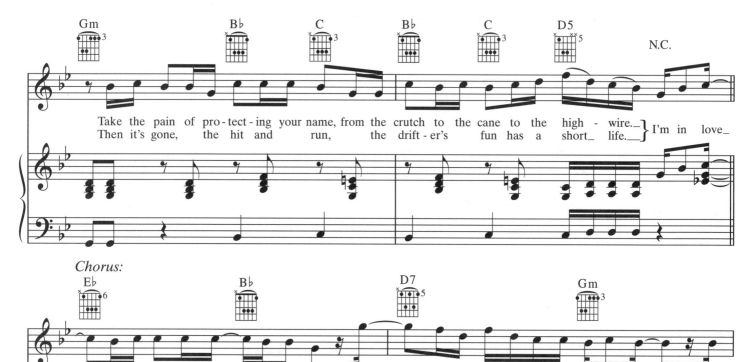

to make love when I wan-na fight. Now some-one un-der-stands me.___ I'm in

love with a___ girl.___ (I'm in love with._) I'm in love with a___ girl.___

(I'm in love with._) I'm in love with a___ girl___ (I'm in love with._) who knows__ me bet - ter. Wants

to make love when I wan-na fight. Now some-one un-der-stands me.___

IN MY ARMS

Words and Music by
TIFFANY LEE ARBUCKLE,
MATT BRONLEEWE and JEREMY BOSE

*Original recording in E♭ minor.

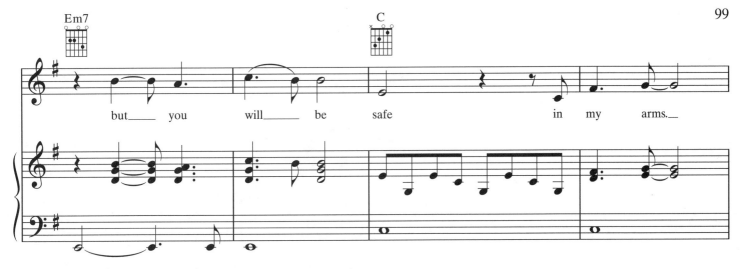

but____ you will____ be safe in my arms.__

Rains__ will pour____down, waves__ will crash a-round, but____ you

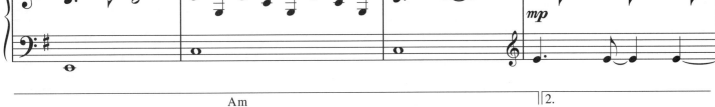

To Coda ⊕ | 1.

will____ be safe in my arms.__

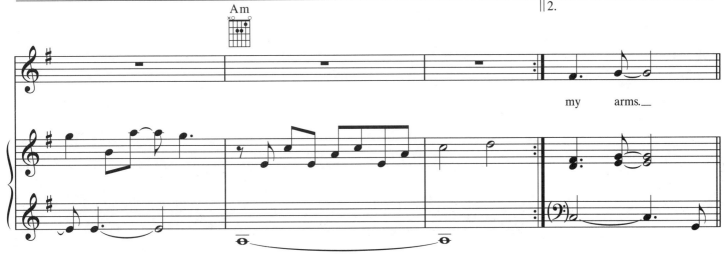

| 2.

my arms.__

Bridge:

Cas - tles, they__ might crum - ble.

Dreams may not__ come true.__ But you are nev - er all

a - lone, 'cause I will al - ways,__

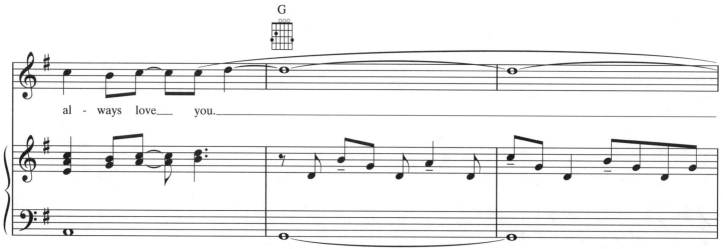

al - ways love__ you.__

D.S. 𝄋 al Coda

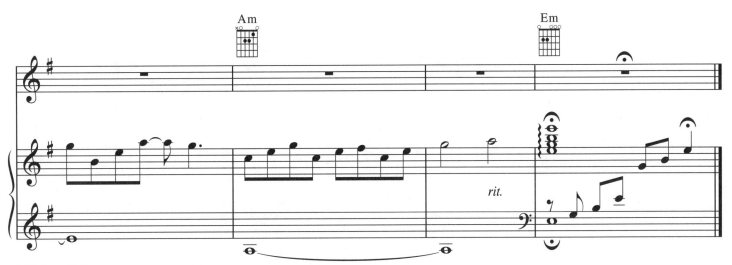

INTO THE NIGHT

Words and Music by
CHAD KROEGER

Moderate rock (♩ = 120)

1. Like a gift____ (1.3.)from the heav - ens, it was eas - y to tell,____ it was love____ from a - bove____ that could save____ me from hell.____ She had fire____
to the puz - zle that falls____ in - to place,____ you can tell____ how we felt____ from the look____ on our fac - es. We were spin -

____ in her soul,____ it was eas - y to see____ how the dev - il him - self____ could be pulled____
ning in cir - cles with the moon____ in our eyes.____ The____ room____ left them mov - ing be - tween____

out of me.___ There were drums___ in the air___ as she start - ed to dance,___ ev-'ry soul_
you and I.___ We for-got___ where we were___ and we lost___ track of time,___ and we sang_

Chorus:

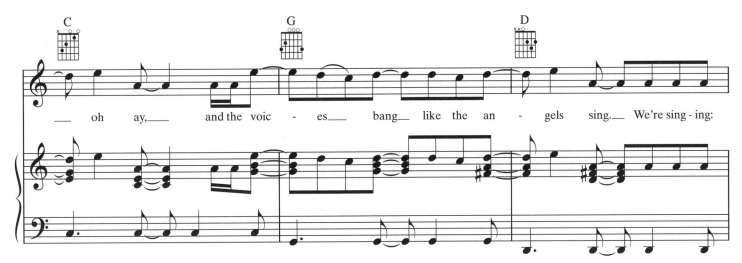

in the room___ keep-ing time___ with their hands.___ } And we sang: Ay oh ay___ oh ay___
to the wind___ as we danced___ through the night.___ }

oh ay,___ and the voic - es___ bang___ like the an - gels sing.___ We're sing-ing:

Ay oh ay___ oh ay___ oh ay,___ and we danced___ on ___ in-to___

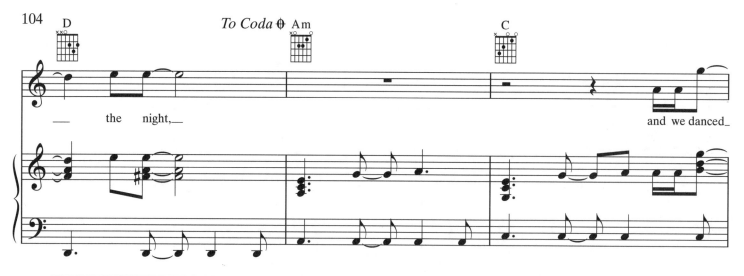

Repeat 4 times

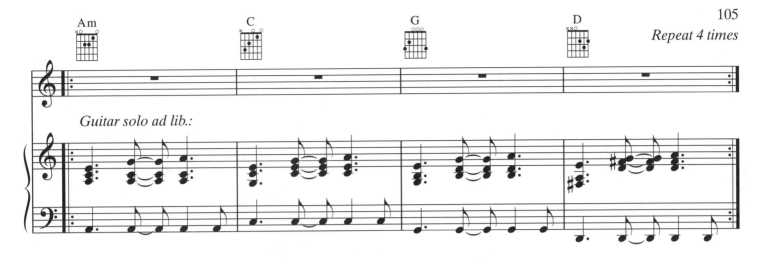

Guitar solo ad lib.:

D.S. %% al Coda

Coda

N.C.

3. Like a gift___

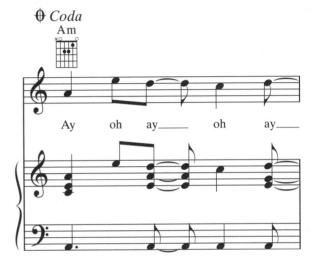

Ay oh ay___ oh ay___

___ oh ay,___ and we danced___ on___ in - to___ the night,___

ay oh ay___ oh ay___ oh ay,___ and we danced___ on___ in - to___

the night,___ ay oh ay___ oh ay___ oh ay,___

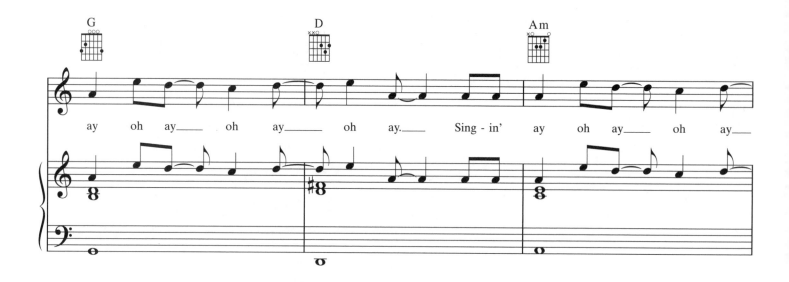

ay oh ay___ oh ay___ oh ay.___ Sing - in' ay oh ay___ oh ay___

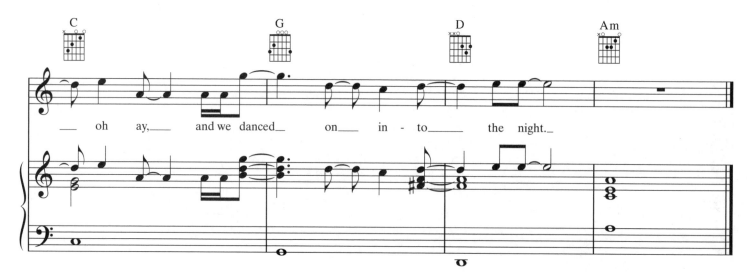

___ oh ay,___ and we danced___ on___ in - to___ the night.___

LAST NAME

Gtr. tuned down 1/2 step:
⑥ = E♭   ③ = G♭
⑤ = A♭   ② = B♭
④ = D♭   ① = E♭

Words and Music by
CARRIE UNDERWOOD, HILLARY LINDSEY
and LUKE LAIRD

Moderately slow country rock ♩ = 80

1. Last night, I got served a lit-tle bit too much of that poi-son, ba-by.
2. We left the club right a-round three o'-clock in the morn-ing. His

Last night, I did things I'm not proud of, and I got a lit-tle cra-zy.
Pin-to sit-tin' there in the park-ing lot, well, it should-'ve been a warn-ing.

Last Name - 8 - 1

...end solo)

Verse 3:

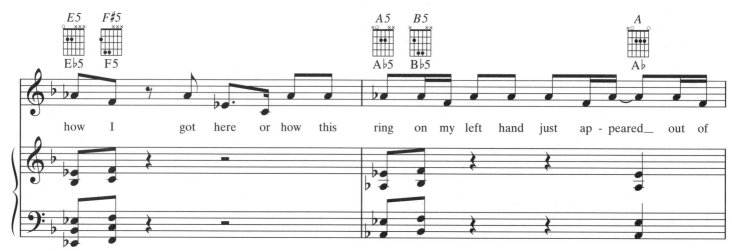

3. To - day, I woke up think-in' 'bout El - vis, some-where in Ve - gas. I'm not sure

how I got here or how this ring on my left hand just ap - peared__ out of

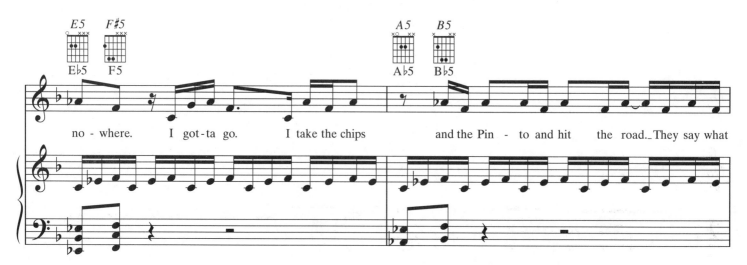

no - where. I got-ta go. I take the chips and the Pin - to and hit the road.__ They say what

turned in - to, "Oh, no, what have I done?" And I____ don't_ e - ven_ know_ my_ last____

___ name. Oh,_____ hey, eh,_____ yeah,_ yeah._

Yeah,_ eh,____ yeah,_ eh,_____ yeah,_ eh,_

yeah,_ eh,_____ yeah,_ eh,____ yeah,_ eh,___ oh._____

_____ It start-ed off, "Hey, Cu-tie, where you from?"_ and then it

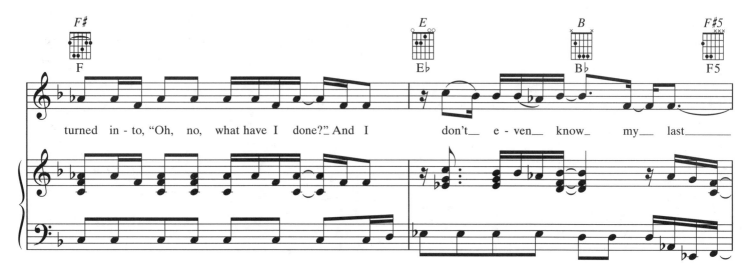

turned in-to, "Oh, no, what have I done?" And I don't_ e-ven_ know_ my_ last_____

Freely

__ name.____ Oh,_____ yeah.____

LOST

Words and Music by
MICHAEL BUBLÉ, ALAN CHANG
and JANN ARDEN

Slow ballad ♩ = 69

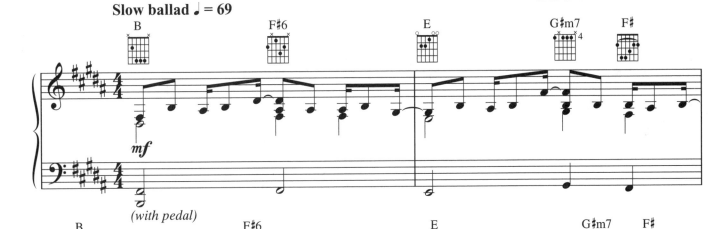

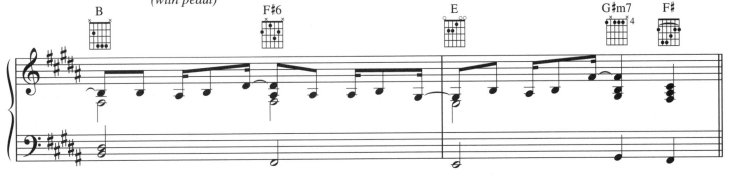

Verse 1:

1. I can't be-lieve it's o-ver; I watched the whole__ thing fall, and I

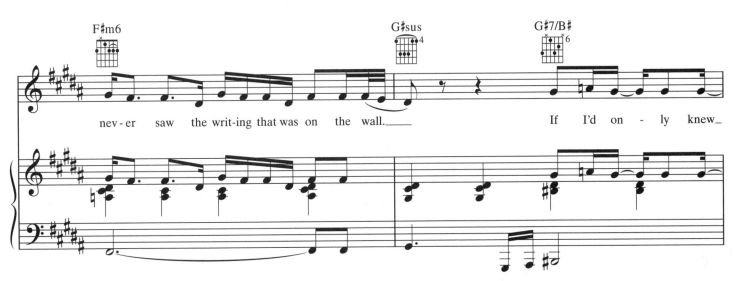

nev-er saw the writ-ing that was on the wall.___ If I'd on-ly knew__

and the dark - ness has won,   babe, you're not lost.____

To Coda

{ When your world's   crash - ing down }
{ When the world's   crash - ing down }

'cause you can't   bear__   the   thought,__

____   I said, babe, you're not   lost.

Verse 3:

3. Life can show no mer - cy;   it can   tear your   soul a - part.   It can

LOVE DON'T LIVE HERE

Words and Music by
DAVID WESLEY HAYWOOD,
CHARLES KELLEY and HILLARY SCOTT

Love Don't Live Here - 7 - 1

Since you walked_ out of____ my door,___ love don't live___ here, love_

____ don't live___ here, girl.____ Oh, love_

____ don't live___ here an - y - more._____

LOVE IS FREE

Words and Music by
SHERYL CROW and
BILL BOTTRELL

*Straight eighths.

Chorus:

Oh, ev-'ry-bod-y, dev-il take your mon-ey. Mon-ey's got no hold on me.__

Oh, oh, ev-'ry-bod-y's mak-ing love 'cause love is free.__

1. 2.

Love is free,__

yeah.___ Love is free._____

MISERY BUSINESS

Words and Music by
HAYLEY WILLIAMS and JOSH FARRO

Gtr. in Drop D, down 1/2 step:
⑥ = D♭　③ = G♭
⑤ = A♭　② = B♭
④ = D♭　① = E♭

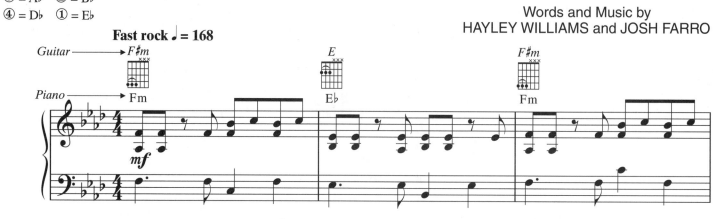

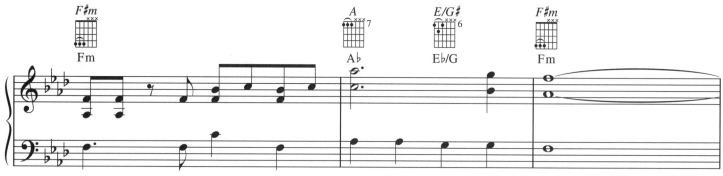

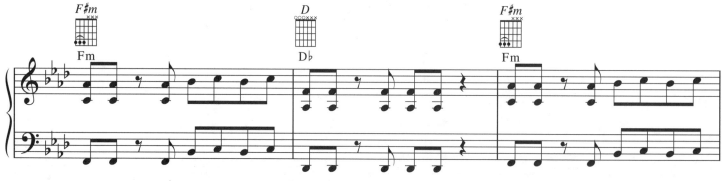

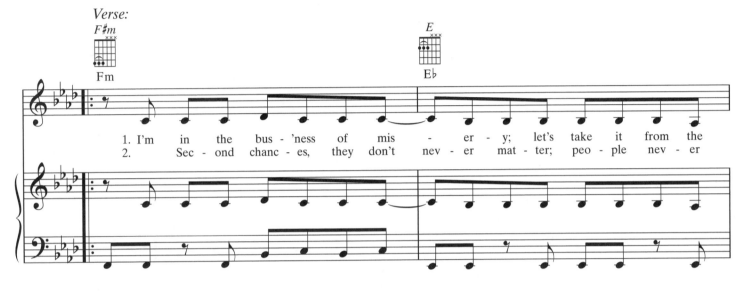

Verse:

1. I'm in the bus – 'ness of mis – – er – y; let's take it from the
2. Sec – ond chanc – es, they don't nev – er mat – ter; peo – ple nev – er

top. She's got a bod – y like an hour – glass; it's tick – ing like a
change. Once a whore, you're noth – ing more. I'm sor – ry; that 'll nev – er

clock. It's a mat – ter of time _____ be – fore we all run out. _____
change. And a – bout for – give – ness _____ we're both sup – posed to have ex –

Just watch my wild-est dreams come true, not one of them in - volv - ing...

Solo:

(Inst. solo ad lib.)

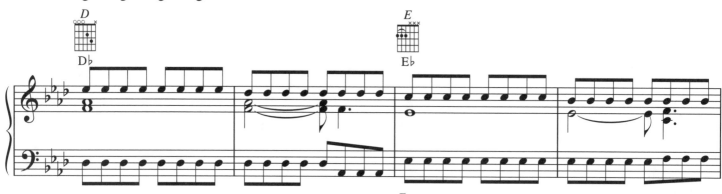

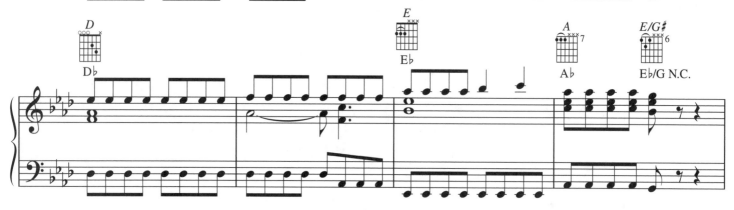

NEW SOUL

Words and Music by
YAEL NAIM and DAVID DONATIEN

Verses 1 & 2:

1. I'm a new soul, I came to this strange world hop - ing I could
young soul in this ver - y strange world, hop - ing I could

learn a bit 'bout how to give and take._ But since I came here, felt the joy and
learn a bit 'bout what is true and fake._ But why all this_ hate? Try to com - mu -

the fear, find - ing my - self mak - ing ev - 'ry pos - si - ble mis - take._
ni - cate, find - ing trust and love is not al - ways eas - y to make._ La la

Chorus:

la la, la la la la la la, la la la la la, la la la, la la

la. La la la la, la la la la la la, la la la la

la, la la la, la la la. 2. See I'm a la. Ooh.

Bridge:

This is a hap - py end,_____ _____ 'cause you don't un - der-stand ev - 'ry-thing you___ have done._____ Now why's ev - 'ry-thing___ so wrong?___

la la la la la la la la la la la la la la la la la la la.

A little slower

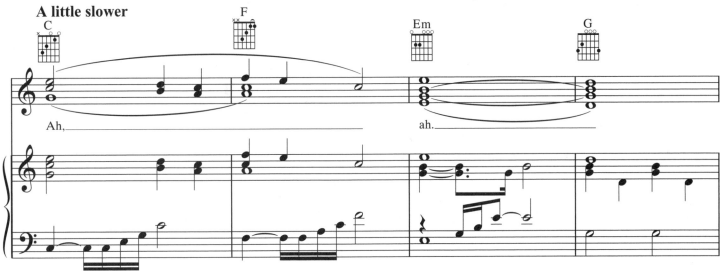

Ah, ah.

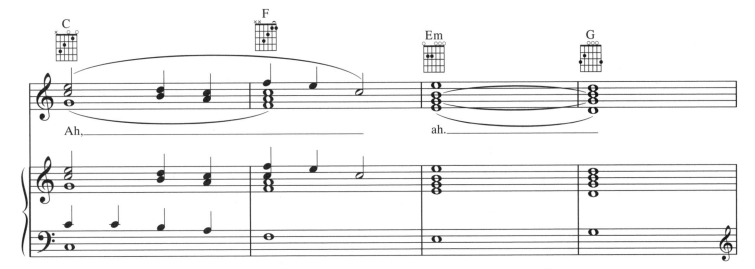

Ah, ah.

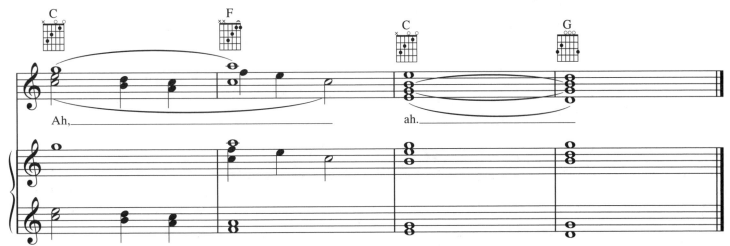

Ah, ah.

OUR TIME NOW

Words and Music by
TOM HIGGENSON, MIKE DALY
and MIA POST

Bright rock ♩ = 192

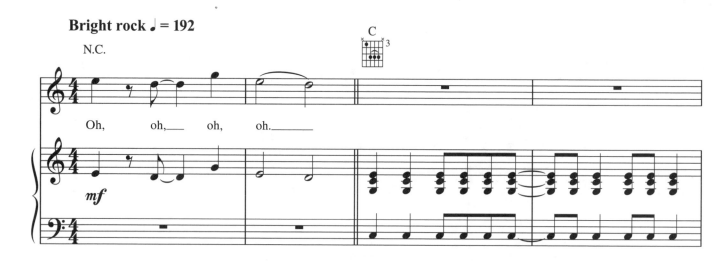

Oh, oh,___ oh, oh._____

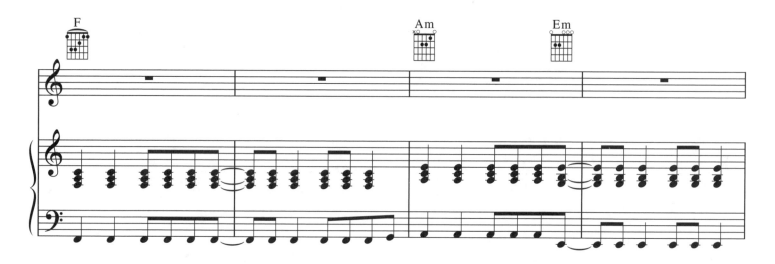

Verse:

1. There will be___ no rules___ to-night,___
2. This is more___ than just___ ro-mance,___

Our Time Now - 5 - 1

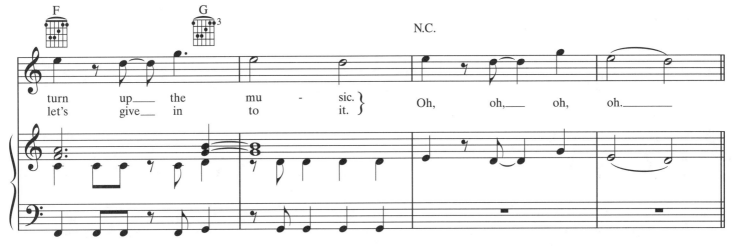

%Chorus:

This is a dance for all___ the lov - ers, tak-ing a chance for one___ an - oth - er.

Fi - nal - ly,___ it's our___ time now.

These are the times that we'll___ re - mem - ber, break-ing the cit-y's heart___ to - geth - er.

To Coda ⊕

Fi - nal - ly,___ it's our___ time now, it's our time

D.S. % al Coda

lov-ers.
(Ah._____)
Oh, oh,___ oh, oh.___ Oh, oh,___ oh, oh.___ Oh, oh,___ oh, oh.___

now._____
(It's our time now.)
It's our time___ now.

(It's our time now._____)
Oh, oh,___ oh, oh.___

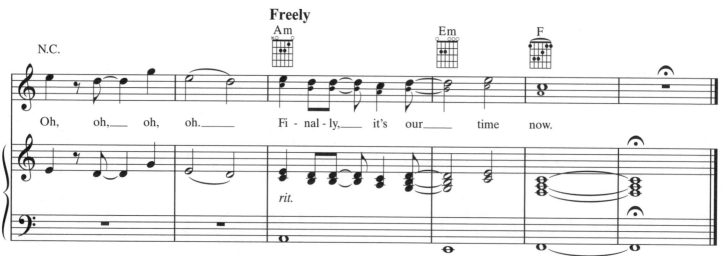

Freely

Oh, oh,___ oh, oh.___ Fi-nal-ly,___ it's our___ time now.

rit.

PARALYZER

Music and Lyrics by
SCOTT ANDERSON, Sean ANDERSON,
RICH BEDDOE, JAMES BLACK and RICK JACKETT

Moderate rock ♩ = 104

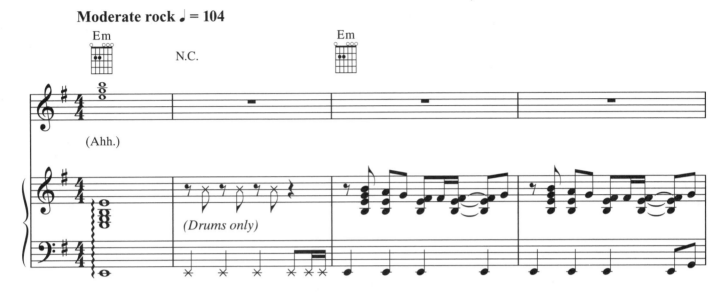

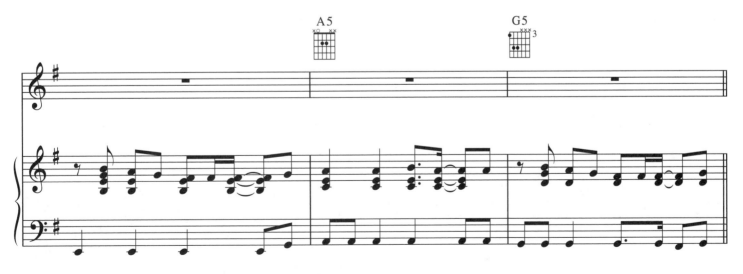

Paralyzer - 6 - 1

Verse:

1. I hold on___ so ner - vous - ly___ to me and my drink.___
2. I hold out___ for one more_ drink_ be - fore_ I think___

I wish__ it was cool - ing___ me._____ But so far___ has
I'm look - ing too des - p'rate - ly._____ But so far___ has

not been_ good.___ It's been s*** - ty,_____ and I
not been_ fun.___ I should been just stay home,_____ if

feel awk - ward as I___ should.___ This club_ has got to_ be_ the most
if one thing real - ly means one.___ This club_ will hope - ful - ly___ be

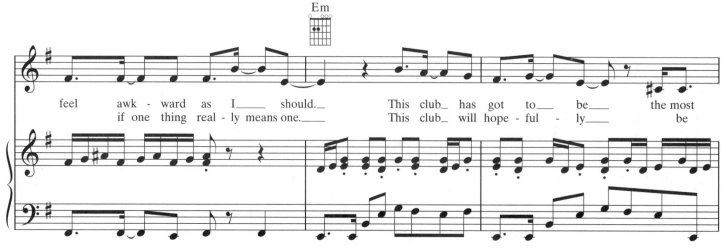

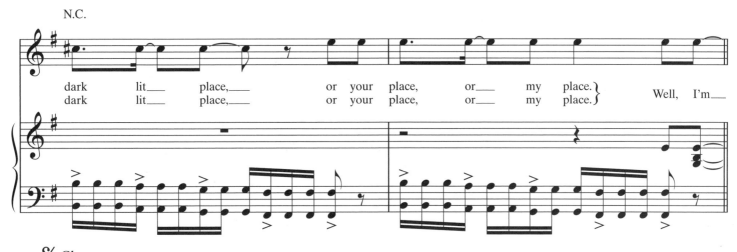

PSYCHO

*All Gtrs. in Drop D, tuned down 1/2 step:
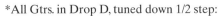
⑥ = D♭   ③ = G♭
⑤ = A♭   ② = B♭
④ = D♭   ① = E♭

Words and Music by
WESLEY SCANTLIN and TONY BATTAGLIA

Moderately fast ♩ = 120

Verse 3:

3. Back in the days___ when we were___ young. When ev-'ry-thing___ ___ was like a load-ed___ gun, read-y to go off at an-y min-ute.___ ___ And you know___ we're gon-na win___ a-gain. May-be I'm the one, may-be I'm the one who is the

Chorus:

RADIO NOWHERE

Words and Music by
BRUCE SPRINGSTEEN

Radio Nowhere - 6 - 1

Verse 3:

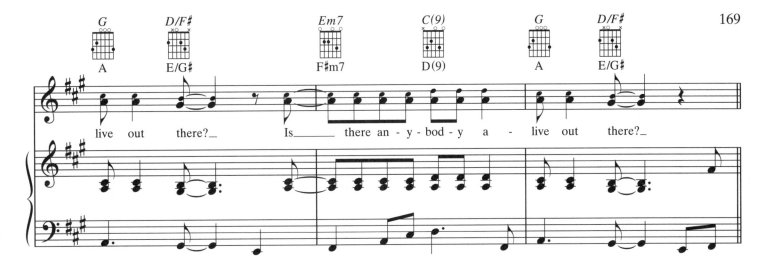

live out there?＿ Is＿ there an - y - bod - y a - live out there?＿

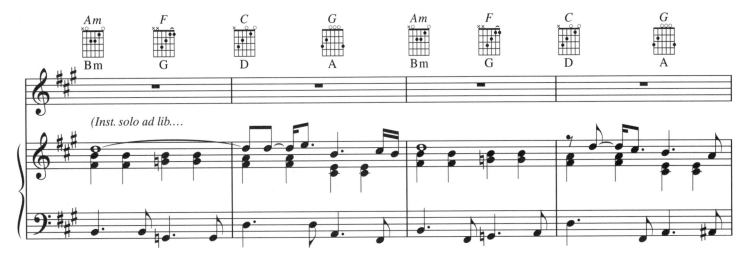

(Inst. solo ad lib....

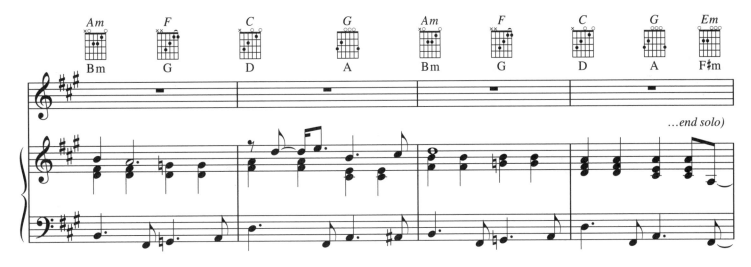

...end solo)

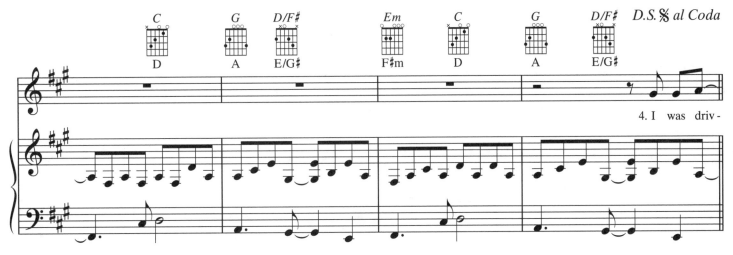

D.S. %al Coda

4. I was driv -

170

ROCKSTAR

Moderately slow ♩ = 76 *Verse 1:*

Lyrics by CHAD KROEGER
Music by NICKELBACK

1. I'm through with stand-ing in line to clubs I'll nev-er get in, it's like the bot-tom of the ninth and I'm nev-er gon-na win. This life has-n't turned out quite the way I want it to be.

(Tell me what you want.) I want a brand-new house on an ep-i-sode of Cribs, and a bath-room I can play base-ball in. And a king-size tub big e-nough for ten plus me.

Rockstar - 6 - 1

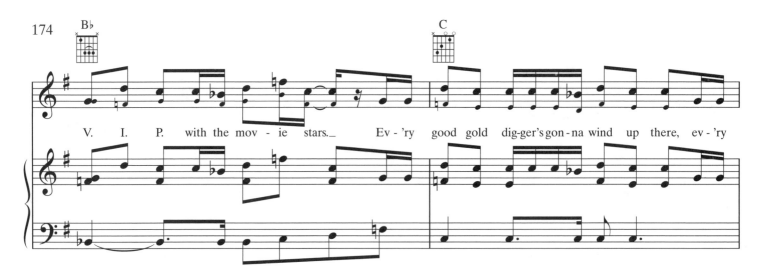

V. I. P. with the mov - ie stars.__ Ev - 'ry good gold dig - ger's gon - na wind up there, ev - 'ry

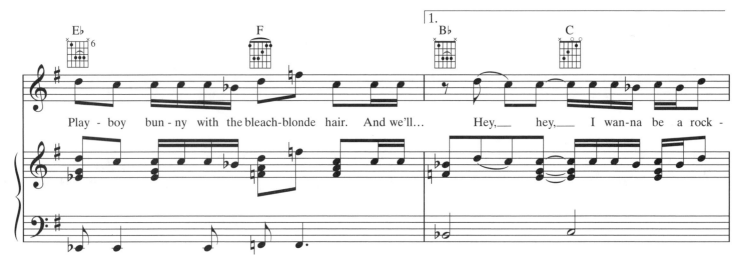

Play - boy bun - ny with the bleach-blonde hair. And we'll... Hey,__ hey,__ I wan-na be a rock-

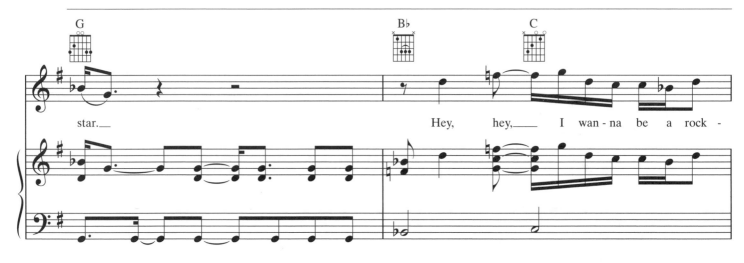

star.__ Hey, hey,__ I wan - na be a rock-

star.__ 3. I wan - na be hide out in the pri - vate rooms__ with the

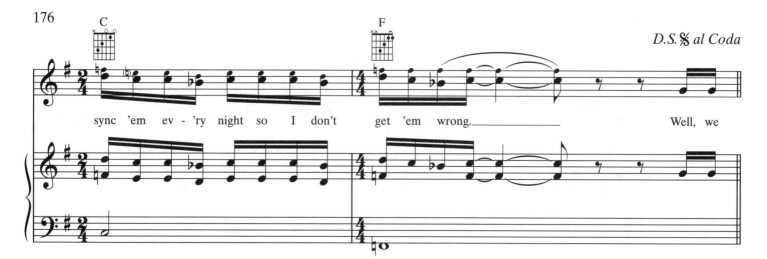

sync 'em ev - 'ry night so I don't get 'em wrong._____ Well, we

Coda

Hey,___ hey,___ I wan-na be a rock - star.___

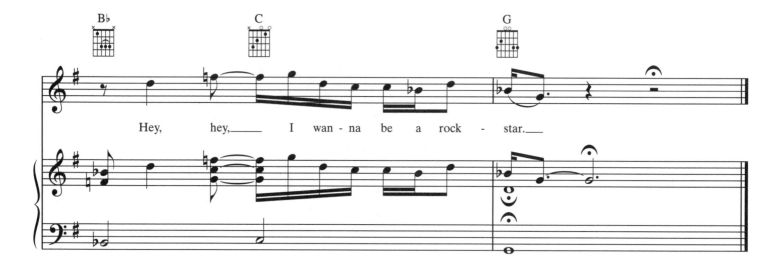

Hey, hey,___ I wan - na be a rock - star.___

Verse 3:
I wanna be great like Elvis, without the tassels,
Hire eight bodyguards who love to beat up assholes.
Sign a couple autographs so I can eat my meals for free. *(I'll have the quesadilla, ha, ha.)*
I'm gonna dress my ass with the latest fashion,
Get a front-door key to the Playboy mansion.
Gonna date a centerfold that loves to blow my money for me. *(So how ya gonna do it?)*
I'm gonna trade this life for fortune and fame,
I'd even cut my hair and change my name.
(To Chorus:)

SO MUCH LOVE

Words and Music by
BRUCE AVARY

So Much Love - 10 - 1

SORRY

Lyrics by
JOSH TODD and
MARTI FREDERIKSEN

Music by
JOSH TODD, KEITH NELSON
and MARTI FREDERIKSEN

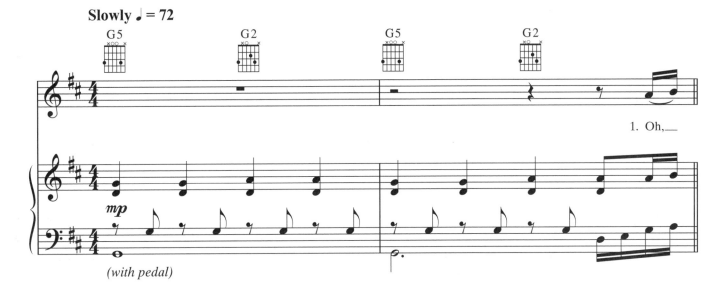

188

Bridge:

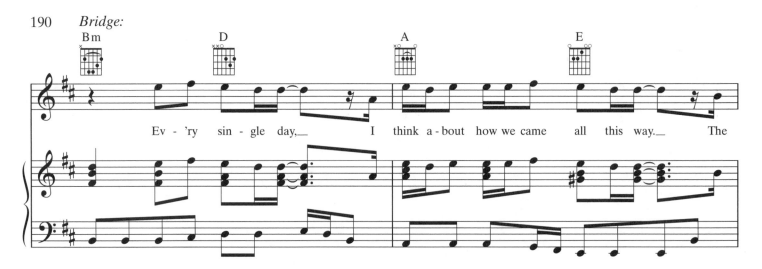

Ev - 'ry sin - gle day,___ I think a - bout how we came all this way.___ The

sleep - less nights_ and the tears_ you cried,_____ it's nev - er too late to make_

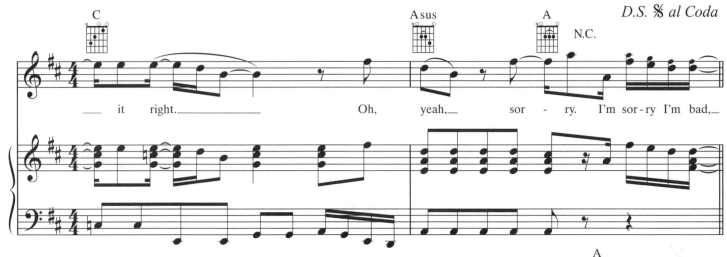

___ it right._____ Oh, yeah,___ sor - ry. I'm sor - ry I'm bad,

D.S. 𝄋 al Coda

Coda

I'm sor - ry._____

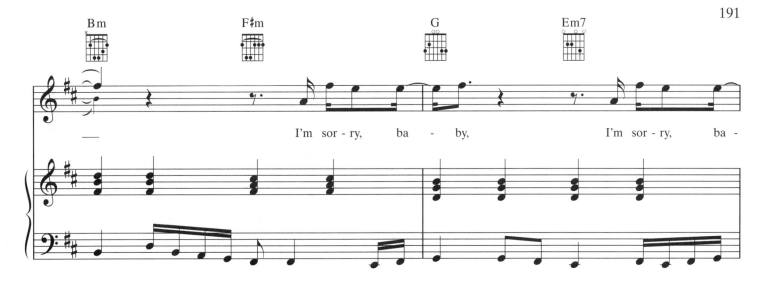

I'm sor - ry, ba - by, I'm sor - ry, ba -

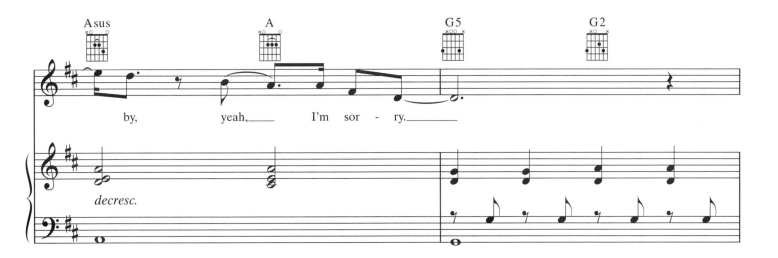

by, yeah,___ I'm sor - ry.___

decresc.

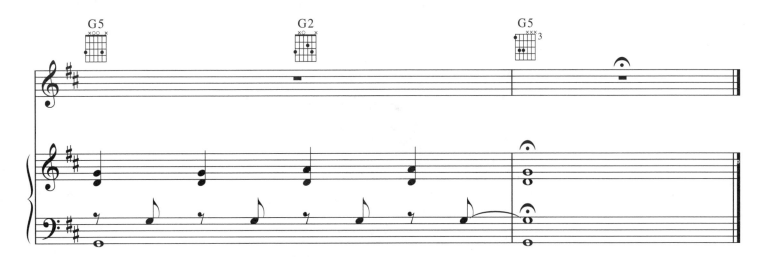

STARLIGHT

Gtr. tuned down 1/2 step:
⑥ = E♭   ③ = G♭
⑤ = A♭   ② = B♭
④ = D♭   ① = E♭

Words and Music by
MATTHEW BELLAMY

Moderately ♩ = 116

Verses 1 & 2:

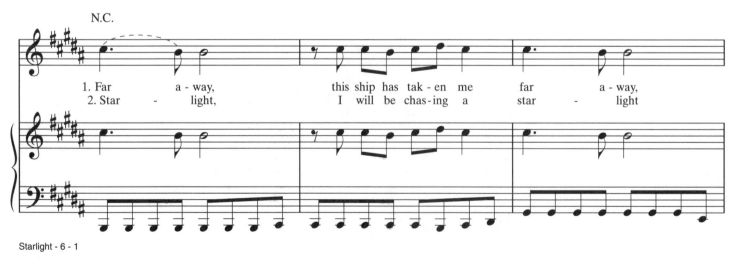

1. Far   a - way,   this ship has tak - en me   far   a - way,
2. Star - light,   I will be chas - ing a   star - light

Starlight - 6 - 1

far a - way from the___ mem - o - ries of the peo - ple who
un-til the end of my___ life._____ I don't know if it's

1. care if I live or___ die.___
2. worth it___ an - y - more._

%Chorus:

C   Dm   Am   F
B   C#m   G#m   E

Hold_____ you in_____ my_____ arms.

C   Dm
B   C#m

I just want - ed__ to__ hold_____ you in_____ my_

SUPERNATURAL SUPERSERIOUS

Moderately fast ♩ = 124

Verse 1:

Words and Music by
PETER BUCK, MIKE MILLS
and MICHAEL STIPE

1. Ev - 'ry - bod - y here comes_ from some - where_ that they would just as soon_ for - get_ and dis - guise. 2. At the sum-

Verses 2 & 3:

Verse 5:

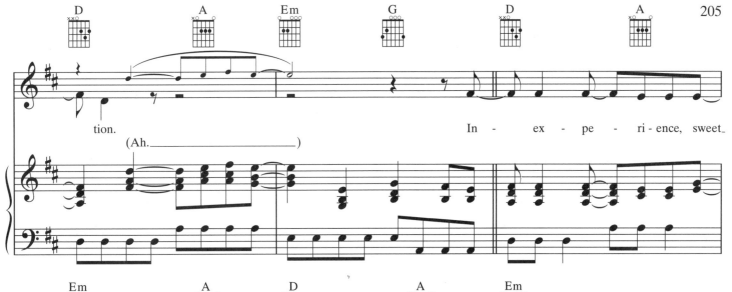

tion. In - ex - pe - ri - ence, sweet

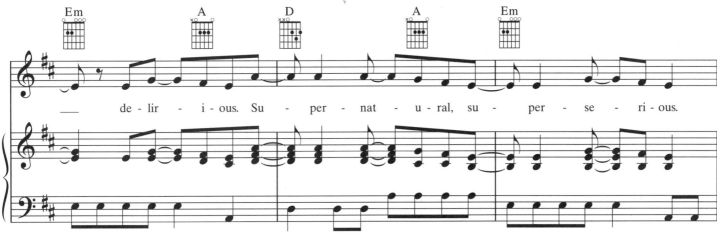

de - lir - i - ous. Su - per - nat - u - ral, su - per - se - ri - ous.

In - ex - pe - ri - ence, sweet_____ de - lir - i - ous. Su -

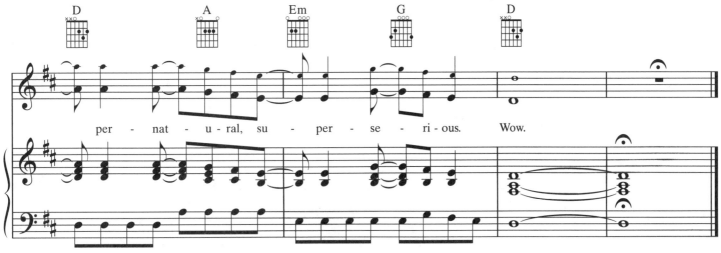

per - nat - u - ral, su - per - se - ri - ous. Wow.

TAKING CHANCES

Words and Music by
KARA DIOGUARDI and
DAVID STEWART

Moderately slow ♩ = 92

Verse 1:

1. Don't know much a - bout your life.

Don't know much a - bout your world,___ but___ don't wan - na be a - lone to - night___ on this plan - et they___ call Earth.___

Taking Chances - 7 - 1

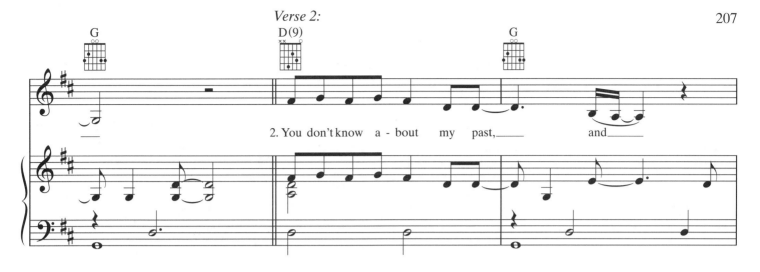

2. You don't know a - bout my past,_____ and_____

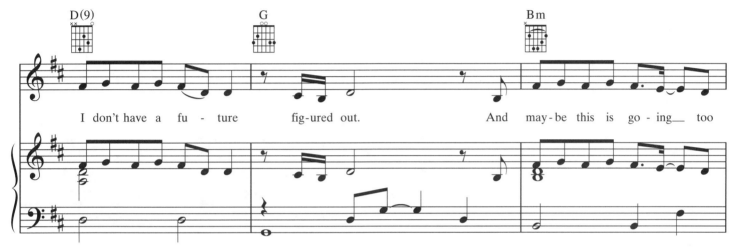

I don't have a fu - ture fig-ured out. And may-be this is go-ing__ too

fast, and may - be it's not meant to last._____

Chorus:

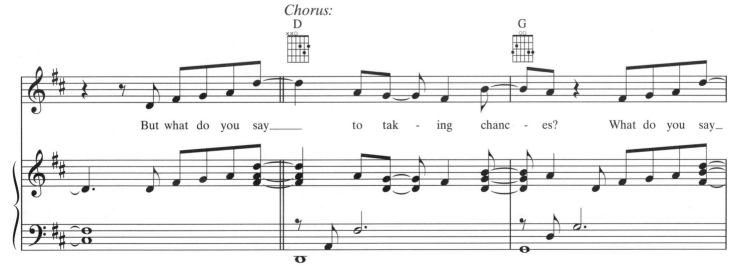

But what do you say_____ to tak - ing chanc - es? What do you say_

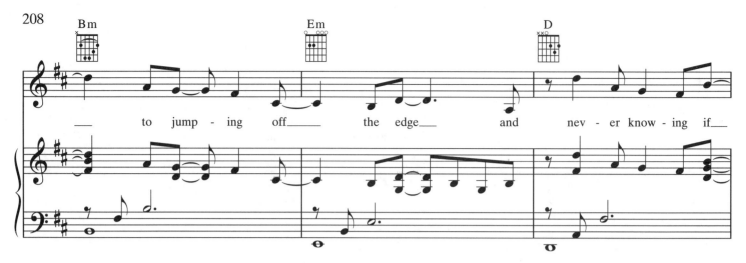

to jump - ing off___ the edge___ and nev - er know - ing if___

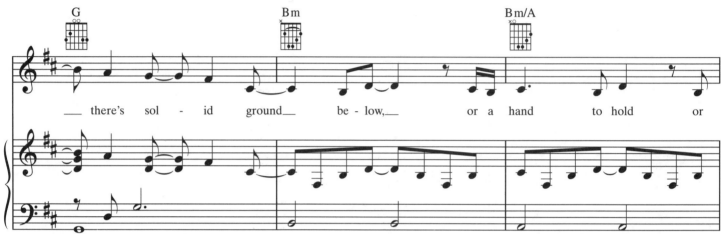

___ there's sol - id ground___ be - low,___ or a hand to hold or

hell to pay?_____ What do you say?_____

cresc.

mf

What do you say?_____

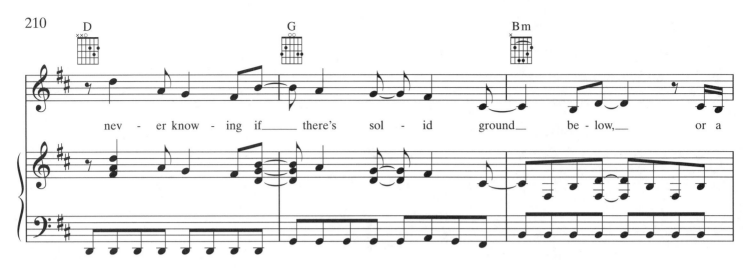

never know-ing if_____ there's sol - id ground_____ be - low,_____ or a

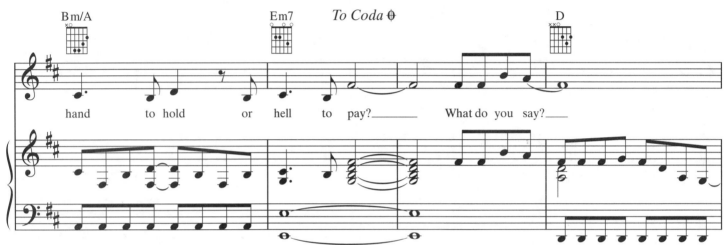

To Coda ⊕

hand to hold or hell to pay?_____ What do you say?_____

What do you say?_____ And_ I had_

Bridge:

___ my heart beat - en down, but I al - ways come back for more,_ yeah. There's

noth-ing like love to pull you up when you're lay-ing down on the floor_ there. So

talk to me, talk to me like lov-ers do. Yeah,

walk with me,_ walk with me like lov - ers____ do,____ like

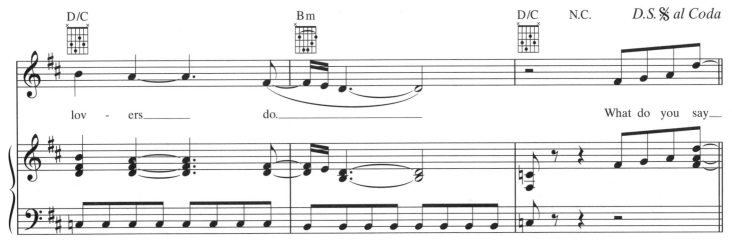

lov - ers____ do.____ What do you say__

Coda

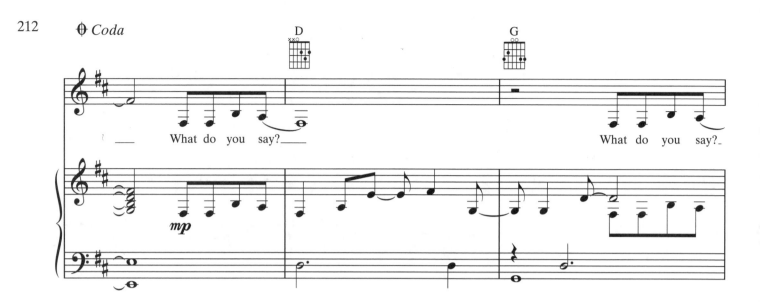

What do you say?___ What do you say?_

Don't know much a-bout your life,___

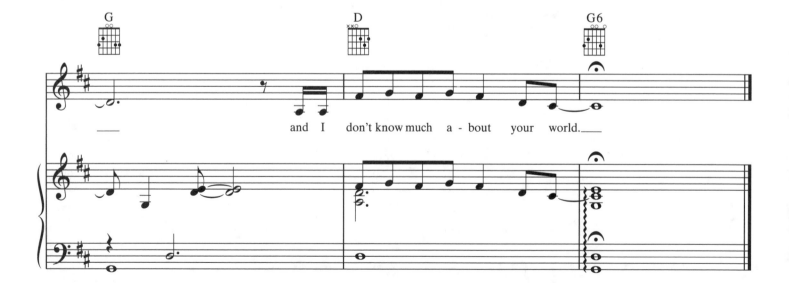

___ and I don't know much a-bout your world.___

TOUCH MY BODY

Words and Music by
TERIUS NASH, CHRISTOPHER STEWART,
MARIAH CAREY and CRYSTAL JOHNSON

Touch My Body - 6 - 1

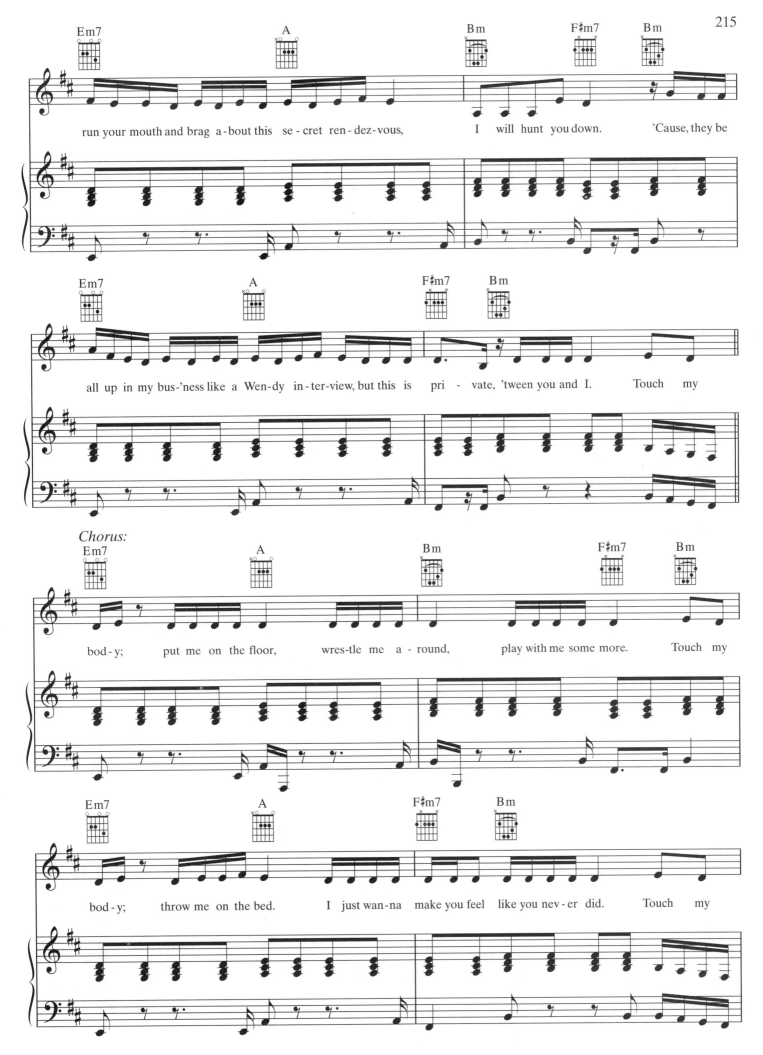

run your mouth and brag a-bout this se-cret ren-dez-vous, I will hunt you down. 'Cause, they be

all up in my bus-'ness like a Wen-dy in-ter-view, but this is pri - vate, 'tween you and I. Touch my

Chorus:

bod - y; put me on the floor, wres-tle me a - round, play with me some more. Touch my

bod - y; throw me on the bed. I just wan-na make you feel like you nev-er did. Touch my

WHATEVER IT TAKES

Words and Music by
JASON WADE and JUDE COLE

220

Chorus:

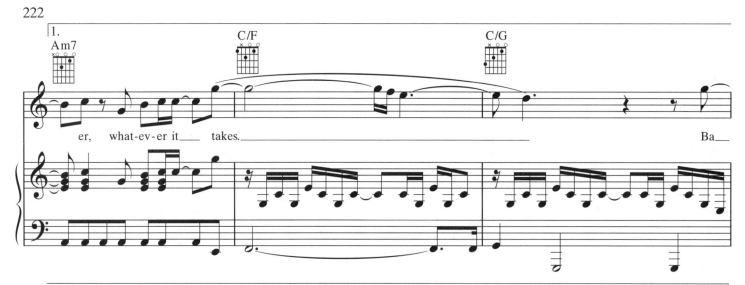

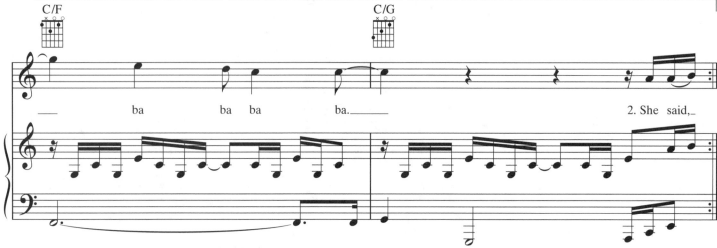

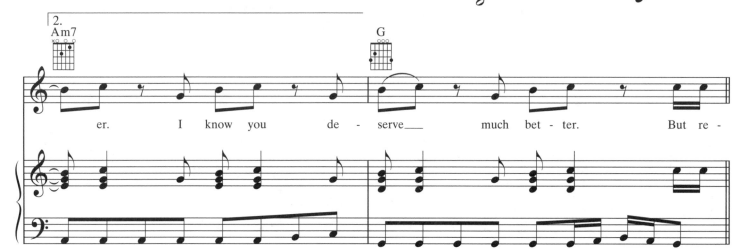

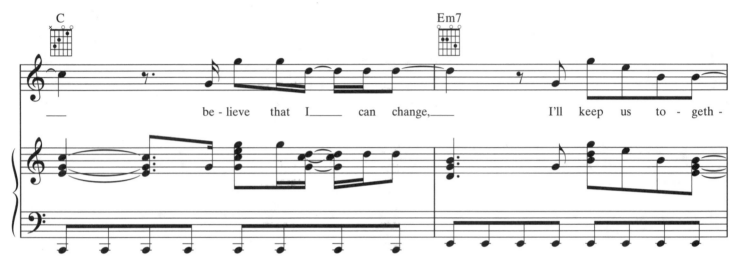